Test Bank to Accompany

Kelly and Lawton

Discovery
An Introduction to Writing

Second Edition

Allyn and Bacon
Boston London Toronto Sydney Tokyo Singapore

TABLE OF CONTENTS

ANSWER KEY

DIAGNOSTIC TEST

Circle the letter of the choice that best completes the sentence or gives a correct statement about the sentence.

SECTION 1: SUBJECTS AND VERBS, SENTENCE FRAGMENTS, COORDINATION, SUBORDINATION, RUN-ON SENTENCES, AND COMMA SPLICES

1. Several of my mother's coworkers are planning a surprise birthday party for her.
    A. subject = coworkers   &   verb = planning
    B. subject = coworkers   &   verb = are planning
    C. subject = several   &   verb = are planning

2. Have you read the article in today's paper about the possibility of life on Mars?
    A. subject = life   &   verb = have read
    B. subject = you   &   verb = have read
    C. subject = article   &   verb = read

3. At early Quaker meetings, the men and women sat on opposite sides of the room.
    A. subject = Quaker meetings   &   verb = sat
    B. subject = men,   &   verb = sat
    C. subject = men, women   &   verb = sat

4. Joan thought about the problem but had no idea how to solve it.
    A. subject = Joan   &   verb = thought, had
    B. subject = Joan   &   verb = thought
    C. subject = problem   &   verb = had thought

5. Until I was twelve and discovered that I could depend on myself.
    A. The group of words is a sentence.
    B. The group of words is not a sentence.

6. The canary escaped.
    A. The group of words is a sentence.
    B. The group of words is not a sentence.

7. Hoping to catch a few bass with his new rod and reel.
    A. The group of words is a sentence.
    B. The group of words is not a sentence.

8. The vase broken before it was even out of the shopping bag.
    A. The group of words is a sentence.
    B. The group of words is not a sentence.

9. _____ the game was played, the umpire flipped a coin to see which team would bat first.
      A. Then
      B. Once
      C. Before

10. Although it was _____ took the kids to the zoo.
      A. raining, we
      B. raining we
      C. raining. We

11. Harold won't buy the _____ asks him to do so.
      A. tickets, unless his dad
      B. tickets. Unless his dad
      C. tickets unless his dad

12. We hung up the beautifully framed _____ the wall still looked bare.
      A. print, and
      B. print, but
      C. print, so

13. They watched the show in different _____ they had just had a big fight.
      A. rooms, since
      B. rooms for
      C. rooms, for

14. Steve and Janet went _____ went out to eat.
      A. shopping, and then they
      B. shopping, then they
      C. shopping and then they

15. At first everyone was nervous, we relaxed when the teacher told a joke.
      A. The sentence is correct.
      B. There is a problem that needs correcting.

16. The players felt grateful to the coach despite the fact that they had lost the game.
      A. The sentence is correct.
      B. There is a problem that needs correcting.

17. Molly's daughter was away at summer _____ house seemed lonely.
      A. camp, the
      B. camp, and the
      C. camp, then the

18. Frankie puts the empty ice cream carton back in the _____ really gets on my nerves.
    A. freezer it
    B. freezer, it
    C. freezer; it

SECTION 2: VERBS, VOICE, TENSES, AND CONSISTENCY

19. Most of my children's friends _____ the same school they do.
    A. attend
    B. attends
    C. has attended

20. At the next meeting, the committee _____ the fundraiser party.
    A. plan
    B. will plan
    C. planned

21. Wendy _____ all through the movie.
    A. cried
    B. cry
    C. will cried

22. Each of Nettie's children _____ one course at the arts center every summer.
    A. taken
    B. take
    C. takes

23. _____ the crew leader of the morning shift of carpenters arrived?
    A. Did
    B. Have
    C. Has

24. By last night, we had _____ them at the mall five times this week.
    A. saw
    B. seen
    C. seeing

25. Your son has not _____ all his lunch, and he wants dessert.
    A. eaten
    B. ate
    C. eat

26. The savings account money was all spent on the new refrigerator.
   A. This sentence has a verb in the active voice.
   B. This sentence has a verb in the passive voice.

27. When Fred called last night, Amy _____ a cake for his birthday.
   A. is baking
   B. was baking
   C. baked

28. All of a sudden her dad comes in and _____, "Fire!"
   A. yelled
   B. yelling
   C. yells

29. I _____ get to sleep last night because I was worried about my son.
   A. couldn't
   B. can't
   C. won't

30. The actors _____ already learning the lines before rehearsals started.
   A. have been
   B. were
   C. been

SECTION 3: NOUNS, PRONOUNS, AND MODIFIERS

31. My kids will not eat either of those _____ of cereal.
   A. kind
   B. kinds

32. Mom called after the departing bus, "Write to your father and _____!"
   A. I
   B. we
   C. me

33. The teacher has asked Kevin and _____ to be partners on the project.
   A. he
   B. him
   C. them

34. Did you know that Oliver and _____ are buying a small boat?
   A. me
   B. us
   C. I

35. The major airlines have reduced _____ fares to New York for the winter.
      A. its
      B. their
      C. our

36. Each of the women gymnasts _____ own gold medal.
      A. have   their
      B. has   their
      C. has   her

37. It has rained five days this week. _____ makes it difficult to keep up the lawn.
      A. This
      B. That
      C. These

38. I get impatient with people who _____ always late.
      A. is
      B. are
      C. were

39. Sandy says that Van Gogh's *Starry Night* is the _____ painting she has ever seen.
      A. beautifulest
      B. most beautiful
      C. more beautiful

40. Corey's mother trains horses so _____ that people from all over Oklahoma hire her.
      A. well
      B. good
      C. better

41. This cold is _____ than the one I had at this same time last year.
      A. worst
      B. bad
      C. worse

42. Vinnie can't _____ remember to take his medicine.
      A. ever
      B. hardly
      C. never

SECTION 4: CAPITALS, PUNCTUATION, SPELLING, AND PARALLEL STRUCTURE

43. Gus works at a _____ station at the edge of the _____.
      A. Texaco . . . Mojave Desert
      B. Texaco . . . mojave desert
      C. texaco . . . Mojave desert

44. Melanie's _____ has written a book that will soon be made into a movie.
      A. Uncle
      B. uncle

45. Jeremy wants to take _____ this semester.
      A. golf, psychology, and spanish
      B. Golf, Psychology, and Spanish
      C. golf, psychology, and Spanish

46. "Stop _____ yelled one twin as the other hit him with the wooden spoon.
      A. it,"
      B. it"!
      C. it!"

47. Leslie asked me if I would take her with me when I go to the _____
      A. store.
      B. store?

48. My mom's cafeteria has three _____ cake, chicken pie, and lasagna.
      A. specialties; carrot
      B. specialties: carrot
      C. specialties carrot

49. The _____ faces were worth over a million dollars each.
      A. model's
      B. models'
      C. models

50. While Tom was at the gym working _____ borrowed his car.
      A. out; Nancy
      B. out Nancy
      C. out, Nancy

51. In Deadwood, South _____ lost their traveler's checks.
      A. Dakota they
      B. Dakota, they

52. Their house, a ninety-five year old log _____ been renovated.
        A. cabin, has
        B. cabin has
        C. cabin – has

53. Tonight at rehearsal he wants only those playing violins, _____ to stay late.
        A. violas, and cellos,
        B. violas and cellos
        C. violas, and cellos

54. Both _____ of the pizza have mushrooms.
        A. halfs
        B. halves

55. Aren't you _____ something very important?
        A. forgetting
        B. forgeting

56. This store will give you a dollar if the clerk neglects to give you a _____.
        A. receipt
        B. reciept

57. _____ is no way _____ car will be ready in time for you to pick it up today.
        A. Their . . . your
        B. There . . . you're
        C. There . . . your

58. In his retirement, my father plans to keep a garden, to build a deck, and _____.
        A. lots of cooking out on the grill
        B. to cook meals out on the grill
        C. grilling food

59. With little money, few materials, and _____, Georgia was still able to build a model of her invention.
        A. almost no encouragement
        B. nobody to encourage her
        C. doing it without encouragement from others

60. Ahmed is a responsible employee, a sensitive husband, and _____.
        A. he loves his children
        B. one whose children are loved
        C. a loving father

CHAPTER 5 – TEST A   SUBJECTS AND VERBS

In each sentence circle the simple or compound subject and underline the verb or verb phrase.

1. The pink clouds in front of the sun made the sky beautiful.

2. Uncle Walter and his wife have lived in the Ozark Mountains all their lives.

3. The simple little house deep in the woods was a peaceful place to visit.

4. That rascal hid my bedroom slipper.

5. Juan and Diane are already planning a small wedding.

6. My cousin still keeps a bird sanctuary in her yard.

7. Nathan's first basketball game will be played tomorrow night.

8. Regular exercise makes me more energetic and keeps the excess pounds off.

9. The huge increase in the number of commuters has caused many traffic jams in our cities.

10. Some of the best chefs never go to formal cooking schools.

11. Her 1982 Toyota wagon looks like a wreck but runs well.

12. Many of the fans in the bleachers have brought binoculars.

13. By next summer, I will have saved enough money for a canoe.

14. The cars in the parking lot are too close together.

15. Sam Nguyen and his brother have just opened a new restaurant.

In the following sentences, circle the simple subject and underline the verb. In the blank to the right, identify the verb as an action verb (ACT) or a linking verb (LV).

16. Tamara seems angry about her daughter's decision.   _____

17. The golf coach and her star player arrived early.   _____

18. On winter nights, a fire in the wood stove feels wonderful.   _____

19. The stew tasted too salty for most of the diners.   _____

20. Our neighbors across the street have a pool.   _____

CHAPTER 5 – TEST B   SUBJECTS AND VERBS

In the paragraph below, circle the simple subject and underline the verb or verb phrase.

(1) Most of us have heard of women such as Clara Barton and Florence Nightingale. (2) These two people made great contributions to nursing education and earned reputations for themselves as pioneers. (3) Even young students frequently recognize the name of scientist Marie Curie. (4) Rachel Carson, a leader in environmental studies, is also known to a generation of Americans. (5) However, many other less famous women have made contributions to science and humanity. (6) For example, Annie Jump Cannon was a leading astronomer. (7) She became a Harvard professor in 1938. (8) She and several women coworkers discovered five thousand new stars. (9) The work of Lise Meitner in physics played an important part in the development of the atomic bomb. (10) Another example is Sonya Kovalesky, a Russian math professor. (11) She studied the movement of an object around a still point and helped with later work in the study of the stars. (12) Other unknown women improved the quality of people's lives. (13) Julia Lathrop served as the first chief of the Children's Bureau of the United States Department of Labor. (14) In the American West, Nellie Cashman organized relief efforts for miners with scurvy during the gold rushes of the 1870s. (15) An organization for the improvement of social conditions was founded by a woman, Margaret Slocum Sage. (16) Many of today's business management practices can be traced to Mary Parker Follett. (17) In the 1920s, Mary Follett was already using team management and cooperative conflict resolution. (18) Some of the women leaders in the areas of art and literature might be more familiar. (19) Mary Cassatt and Georgia O'Keeffe have certainly added to the beauty of our world. (20) Today, many organizations celebrate the achievements of great women and educate the public about their contributions.

CHAPTER 6 – TEST A   SENTENCE FRAGMENTS

Write S in the blank beside each complete sentence. Write F beside each fragment. In the space provided, rewrite each fragment as a complete sentence, adding or changing words as needed.

_____1. Climbing the crepe myrtles in their backyard.

_____2. Knowing the weeds in the flower bed had to be pulled, she got up early.

_____3. The Lewis and Clark expedition the first explorers in several of our western states.

_____4. Under the beach umbrella to avoid getting sunburned.

_____5. While Jeff painted the ceiling and Mark fixed lunch.

_____6. It arrived in the mail yesterday.

_____7. To go white water rafting down the Colorado River.

_____8. Quilting was my great aunt's hobby and joy.

_____9. Outrageously overpriced in the specialty stores.

_____10. Rachel, a gifted organist who accompanies our choir.

_____11. Listen to the eerie howl of that wind.

_____12. Kim, a young mother of twins and a full-time nurse, also volunteers for the Red Cross.

_____13. Until I can find a suitable babysitter.

_____14. Without even trying to repair the broken chair.

_____15. On the rug next to the fireplace lay a white cat.

For each of the following fragments, write in the blank what is needed to form a complete sentence. Label as follows:
    V   if it needs a verb
    HV   if it needs a helping verb
    S   if it needs a subject
    CI   if it needs a new complete idea

16. Wants to become a surgical technician.   _____

17. The bowl broken into two large pieces.   _____

18. As Julio walked into the doctor's office.   _____

19. The last thing on her mind during the test.   _____

20. Once upon a time in a country far away.   _____

CHAPTER 6 – TEST B   SENTENCE FRAGMENTS

Label each word group F if it is a fragment or S if it is a complete sentence. Then, revise this passage to correct each fragment. You can join them to other sentences or add words to make them into complete sentences. Be sure to use correct punctuation and capitalization. Write your corrections above the lines.

1. _____

2. _____

3. _____

4. _____

5. _____

6. _____

7. _____

8. _____

9. _____

10. _____

11. _____

12. _____

13. _____

14. _____

15. _____

16. _____

17. _____

18. _____

19. _____

20. _____

(1) One of the fondest memories I have of my childhood spending a week at Grandma's house in the country. (2) She lived on a small farm. (3) With a big vegetable garden and an old rickety barn. (4) A reminder of the days when mules helped run the farm. (5) Feeling like pioneer girls in the Old West. (6). My sister and I playing for hours in the ancient wagon. (7) Working was also a major part of any visit to Grandma's. (8) Hoed corn, shelled peas, and picked green beans. (9) We explored the damp, dark basement. (10) Where row after row of canned vegetables and pickles stood, souvenirs of the past. (11) Taking a break every morning to watch Grandma's favorite "story" on television. (12) There was one daily chore that we fought for the privilege of doing and usually ended up doing together. (13) Going to the post office. (14) Which was actually located in a special neighbor's house down the road. (15) Evenings spent on the porch, hearing funny tales of my dad's childhood, were so special. (16) Time flew. (17) Even as teenagers, my sister and I loved summer weeks on Grandma's farm. (18) Although perhaps for different reasons. (19) Gaining a personal experience of my family's own history. (20) A precious gift in my adulthood.

CHAPTER 7 – TEST A   SUBORDINATION

Underline each main clause contained in the sentences below. Circle each subordinate clause. In the blank, write S if the sentence is simple or CX if the sentence is complex.

1. Many visitors enjoy the mild weather in San Diego all year.   _____
2. When it rains, the busy streets are full of umbrellas.   _____
3. You should never sign a contract until you have carefully read the fine print.   _____
4. Bill and Lindsay often go out to eat at the newest ethnic restaurants. _____
5. The woman that I called just now is a landscape architect.   _____

Using the subordinating conjunction in parentheses, combine each of the following pairs of ideas. Punctuate the complex sentences correctly. Write your sentences on the lines provided.

6. Gene went to the checkout line.
    He had bought everything on his list.   (when)
    _____

    _____

7. You will not be allowed to go to the park.
    You finish your homework.   (until)
    _____

    _____

8. I bought the jacket.
    I discovered it was ripped.   (after)
    _____

    _____

9. Marcy has taken so many days off.
    She is almost out of vacation time.   (since)
    _____

    _____

10. Everyone in the family is allergic to poison ivy.
    They all went walking in the dense woods.   (although)
    _____

    _____

Add either a subordinate clause or a complete idea to turn each word group into a logical complex sentence.

11. As Paula locked her office door, _____

_____

12. I will be glad to type the report _____

_____

13. The man _____ is my uncle.

14. If I won the state lottery, _____

_____

15. I really like a book _____

_____

Where they are needed, insert commas in the sentences below. If a sentence does not need a comma, write C beside it.

16. Until their homework is finished Sally and her brother aren't allowed to ride the horses.

17. My mother who went to beauty college in Texas now has a salon of her own.

18. Karla is working late again because the deadline is tomorrow.

19. The design that you turned in was chosen as first prize winner.

20. If the turtle is disturbed by noise or lights she will not lay her eggs.

CHAPTER 7 – TEST B   SUBORDINATION

Underline each subordinate clause. If the sentence does not contain a subordinate clause, write S (for simple sentence) above it.

(1) A fun family vacation can involve a great deal of work. (2) Before the loaded-down minivan or car leaves home, many decisions about the trip and arrangements must be made. (3) Deciding where to go in the first place isn't easy if you have family members with different interests. (4) One person might love the beach while another person prefers to visit a city. (5) Those in charge of the planning must consider things such as weather, entertainment or educational opportunities, and budget. (6) Compromise and foresight are two essential elements of deciding the destination. (7) After the place is determined, the rest of the planning begins. (8) A parent who is in charge of arranging all the details can be tired before the trip even starts.

Use an appropriate subordinating conjunction to join each of the following pairs of ideas into one sentence. Add subordinating conjunctions and commas as needed above the line. Change periods or capitals as needed.

(9) Most families with children take their vacations in the summer. Kids are out of school. (10) Summer vacations might be a bit more difficult to plan. Roads, hotels, campgrounds, and parks are busiest then. (11) Reservations can help prevent disappointment and frustration. Reservations can be made in advance. (12) Planning details might sound like work. It can lay the foundation for a better time together. (13) A family is preparing a trip. It's a good idea to let each person talk about what would make it fun.

Proofread each sentence for proper comma usage. Correct by adding commas as needed above the line.

(14) If family members enjoy very different activities you should try to provide some of each kind of activity. (15) Travel agents who can provide ideas about activities in a certain place help family members anticipate and plan for their time together. (16) A way to avoid misunderstandings is to lay down a few general rules that will help everyone know what is expected. (17) Share the meal or housekeeping duties while you are away from home. (18) If you invest some time in careful planning your vacation will be more pleasant as a result.

In the space below, write two complex sentences of your own about a vacation you have taken. Make sure each sentence contains a subordinate clause.

19. _____

_____

20. _____

_____

CHAPTER 8 – TEST A   COORDINATION

Fill in each blank with a coordinating conjunction or a conjunctive adverb that makes sense.
Read each sentence carefully for punctuation clues on which kind of word to insert.

1. Most of the roads on the way were not paved, _____ Mike's car got very dirty.
2. They turned on the large window fan, _____ the room remained hot.
3. I may pack the car tonight, _____ I may wait until tomorrow morning.
4. Sofia was visiting relatives in Mexico last month; _____, she could not come to the party.
5. Maine is beautiful in the fall; _____, it can be quite cold.

Combine each of the following pairs of sentences using coordinating conjunctions. Write your compound sentences on the lines below, being sure to use capitals and punctuation correctly.

6. The state's bridges must be repaired.
    Our highway infrastructure will be dangerous.

    _____

    _____

7. Roger has a large snowblower.
    His drive is always clean.

    _____

    _____

8. A volt is a unit of electrical power.
    An ohm is a unit of electrical resistance.

    _____

    _____

9. Women began to fight for the vote in the 1840's.
    They did not win that right until 1920.

    _____

    _____

10. Herb's favorite shoes are completely worn out.
    He walks miles in them everyday.

    _____

    _____

On the lines provided, add words to create compound sentences. Read each sentence carefully for clues to help you create logical sentences.

11. Her neighbors keep their lights on all night, yet _____

_____.

12. Lars bought the boat with his own money, so _____

_____.

13. Taking a study skills class may help you manage your time; furthermore, _____

_____.

Proofread these sentences for errors in the use of commas and semicolons. Insert the missing punctuation marks above the lines.

14. Butch's day-care job doesn't pay well however he loves working with the children.

15. The sunrise at Key West is beautiful and the atmosphere is relaxed.

16. Her reply is clear there can be no doubt about her feelings toward him.

17. My speedometer is not working properly so I cannot tell how fast I am driving.

18. Howard Hughes was an extremely wealthy man but was he happy?

19. It rained one day during our trip otherwise the weather was perfect.

20. I need a new job I cannot stand the one I have.

CHAPTER 8 – TEST B   COORDINATION

Fill in each blank with a coordinating conjunction or a conjunctive adverb. Read each sentence carefully for punctuation clues on which type of word to use.

(1) Today there are over 200 known breeds of dogs, _____ all of these descended from only one animal, the wolf. (2) Dogs were first domesticated around 10,000 years ago; _____, there have been many generations for specific breeds to be created. (3) Some breeds were designed for certain looks or temperaments, _____ some were intended to do jobs around a home or farm. (4) Dogs could be workers, _____ they could be companions. (5) There are only six official classes of purebred dogs; _____, there are thousands of mixtures possible.

Combine the following pairs of simple sentences with coordinating conjunctions. Insert commas and conjunctions above the line.

(6) Dogs of mixed breeds are officially called mongrels. Those who love them call them pets. (7) Those who raise purebred dogs go to shows. They can show their dogs and compete for prizes. (8) Paintings of dogs appear near those of people in ancient Egyptian tombs. We know that dogs were considered pets in those times.

Proofread the following sentences for errors in punctuation. Correct the sentences by inserting correct punctuation above the line.

(9) Dogs see the world differently than people do objects look the same to them in darkness and in daylight. (10) Their hearing range is also very different therefore they can hear pitches that humans cannot hear. (11) Some breeds are especially intelligent indeed dogs have been trained to guide the blind or help quadriplegic patients. (12) Anyone who has loved a dog knows that dogs communicate with their body language but a person has to know what certain signs mean. (13) A dog will wag its tail to show a friendly greeting or it will go down on its

forepaws with its back end high to say, "Let's play!" (14) A beloved dog will help its owner relax furthermore studies show that a person's blood pressure actually lowers when talking to a pet. (15) At Christmas or on children's birthdays, many folks will adopt an adorable puppy however they should remember that puppies grow up to be dogs. (16) One should think seriously about the responsibilities of caring for a mature dog otherwise the cute puppy may wind up at a pound. (17) A dog can herd livestock for a rancher or it can provide security to an elderly person who lives alone. (18) However, most people own dogs for a different reason usually a person owns a dog to have a loyal friend.

On the lines below, write two compound sentences about any dog you have known. Make sure each of your sentences contains two complete ideas. Punctuate correctly.

19. _____

_____

20. _____

_____

CHAPTER 9 – TEST A   AVOIDING COMMA SPLICES AND RUN-ON SENTENCES

Proofread for errors in sentence combination. In the blank, write C beside a correct sentence, RO beside a run-on, or CS beside a comma splice.

_____ 1. My college roommate Philip is now a playwright he lives and works in New York City.

_____ 2. All the children in the day-care center take naps after lunch, it's the only quiet time of the day.

_____ 3. Keeping a journal is an effective way to overcome the anxiety that many new writers feel.

_____ 4. Before work, Sheila starts her day at the gym with a workout.

_____ 5. Hang gliding began in California in the late 1960s, also known as sky surfing, it is most popular on the coast.

_____ 6. Dag Hammarskjold won the Nobel Peace Prize in 1961 he was killed in a plane crash that year while on a trip for the United Nations.

_____ 7. Shakespeare wrote plays about historical figures, for example, there really was a king of Scotland named MacBeth.

_____ 8. Frank and Trudie work in their garden every weekend, and all the neighbors enjoy their results.

_____ 9. Katie's friend from Australia visited last year now she plans to go there for a few months.

_____ 10. Best known today as a poet, Wallace Stevens was also an insurance executive.

_____ 11. Nancy will be playing her own music at the coffeehouse this is her first public appearance in our area.

_____ 12. I cannot seem to find my keys, have you seen them?

Proofread for run-on sentences or comma splices. Correct errors using punctuation, coordination, or subordination. Write the corrected sentences on the lines provided. If the sentence is correct, write "Correct" on the line.

13. James will attend school to be an optician he has always wanted to help people see better.

_____

_____

14. Pam's parents are moving to a nursing home, they can no longer take care of themselves.

_____

_____

15. There were no seats left in the auditorium Don stood in the back to see the show.

_____

_____

16. Hobbling along on her crutches, Tara tried to keep up with the others.

_____

_____

17. New Orleans is a wonderful place to visit there is jazz music and great Creole cooking.

_____

_____

Correct this run-on sentence three ways, according to the specific instructions below. Write each correction on the lines provided. Be sure to punctuate correctly.

Sam dyed his hair blue his parents are not too upset.

18. with a coordinating conjunction

_____

_____

19. with a semicolon

_____

_____

20. with a subordinating conjunction

_____

_____

CHAPTER 9 – TEST B   AVOIDING COMMA SPLICES AND RUN-ON SENTENCES

The following passage contains some run-ons and comma splices. Make corrections by adding conjunctions, punctuation, and capitalization as necessary above the line. Write C above each correct sentence.

(1) Have you ever wondered when some of our most common everyday items were invented you might be surprised to know how long some of these have been around. (2) Television has been around since 1926 a color image was transmitted only three years later, in 1929. (3) Our desk drawers contain some inventions from early this century. (4) Cellophane for tape originated in 1908, paper clips date back to 1900. (5) Carbon paper goes all the way back to 1806. (6) Some of the household tools we use have a long history flashlights have shone since 1891 the electric hand drill was invented in 1895. (7) Although they weren't commonly used until much later, contact lenses were first created in 1887, hearing aids date back to 1880. (8) It may surprise you to learn that the use of microfilm, fluorescence, and the steam-powered airship all began in 1852. (9) Your track coach's stopwatch has been around since 1855 your great grandmother's sewing machine might be an original 1846 model. (10) The next time you turn up the air conditioning with the thermostat or mow your yard, think of the year 1830 that's when these activities became possible. (11) Scientists have known about he caffeine in your coffee since 1821 and the sodium in your potato chips since 1807. (12) Let's not overlook the flush toilet it was invented in 1778!

Write C in the blank beside each correct sentence. Write CS beside each comma splice or RO beside each run-on.

_____ 13. Other inventions might surprise you for a different reason.

_____ 14. It may seem that some familiar devices have been around forever, they are actually inventions of the past few decades.

_____ 15. DNA fingerprinting was first used in 1986 the megabit computer chip of 1984 is a relative newcomer.

_____ 16. Most of us own CD players these have been around only since 1984, and the CD-ROM which we use on our computers is from 1985.

_____ 17. We have heard of "test tube babies" for years, the first child developed from a frozen embryo was born in 1985.

_____ 18. Even while you are completing this test, inventors are developing products and processes that will soon be a part of our everyday lives.

Correct this run-on in two different ways. Write your sentences in the lines below.

Inventors improve our world we should give them credit.

19. _____

_____

20. _____

_____

CHAPTER 10 – TEST A   SUBJECT-VERB AGREEMENT

Underline the subject and circle the correct verb in each of the sentences of the following passage.

(1) Sports (remains/remain) a dominant part of U.S. popular culture. (2) As they have for years, people from all walks of life (follows/follow) the progress of their favorite teams. (3) In most major U.S. cities, the home team (enjoys/enjoy) great support from the public. (4) Also, with the availability of cable and satellite systems today, everybody with a few extra dollars (has/have) the opportunity to see far more games than ever before.

(5) The sales figures for clothing bearing the logo of a professional team also (illustrate/illustrates) American's on-going love affair with sports. (6) There (is/are) a team jersey or hat in many wardrobes throughout the country. (7) Economics (doesn't/don't) lie; millions of people pay plenty just so they can wear items like their favorite stars.

(8) In addition, over the last decade, interest in sports memorabilia (has/have) continued to grow. (9) There (has/have) been many published accounts of individuals who became rich after finding a valuable baseball card at a yard sale somewhere. (10) (Doesn't/Don't) everyone today know the potential value of old baseball cards?

(11) National exposure provided by cable broadcasters like ESPN and MTV (has/have) produced a whole new generation of superstars: extreme athletes. (12) Today's new pros (doesn't/don't) hit homeruns or score goals. (13) For these athletes, a skateboard or a special bike (is/are) required equipment. (14) Both the X-Games and the Gravity Games (has/have) drawn the attention of millions to these extreme athletes.

(15) Anybody who thinks these people aren't athletes obviously (has/have) never watched them perform. (16) (Has/Have) these critics ever tried to ride straight up a ramp, do a flip in the

air, and continue riding? (17) Strength and agility (is/are) vital to these athletes, just as they are for other top professionals. (18) An event such as street luge, with participants careening down steep, winding hills, flat on their backs, on a platform slightly larger than a skateboard, (calls/call) for toughness and courage.

(19) Clearly, both traditional and extreme sports (continues/continue) to hold the public's interest. (20) Thanks to extensive media coverage, fans of both kinds of sports (has/have) plenty of opportunity to cheer on their favorites.

CHAPTER 10 – TEST B   SUBJECT-VERB AGREEMENT

Each sentence in the following passage contains an error in subject-verb agreement. Correct the errors by crossing out the incorrect verb and writing the correct verb form above the incorrect one.

(1) NASA scientists studying Mars has recently discovered evidence suggesting that water may exist on our neighboring planet. (2) The new theories about this vital fluid is based on pictures transmitted by the Mars Global Surveyor. (3) The most recent images, up to 10 times sharper in focus than earlier pictures, shows deep gullies and channels, evidence of water flowing.

(4) There have long been speculation about the existence of water on Mars. (5) Even today, some people, like the early astronomers, believes the lines visible on the planet's surface are canals. (6) In more modern times, however, scientists has proven that the idea of canals on Mars is science fiction, not science.

(7) Still, the various features of the Red Planet's landscape continues to inspire the idea of water at some past time. (8) The latest evidence strengthen these theories of water on Mars. (9) A key feature of the newest findings are that the channels and gullies lack impact craters and other signs associated with millions of years of existence. (10) In fact, the gullies and channels in the recent photos seems relatively recent.

(11) Researchers studying the issue argues that water caused these geographical features. (12) But if there are water, where is it? (13) The extreme temperatures on Mars makes surface water impossible because it would either freeze or boil away. (14) Some experts therefore believes that the water lies beneath the surface of the planet.

(15) The prospect of water on Mars excite scientists because of the many implications and possibilities. (16) For example, the presence of subsurface water in sufficient quantities mean

that life forms similar to forms on earth may have existed. (17) Also, in water there are the essence of two potent rocket fuels, oxygen and hydrogen, so explorers would have what they need to make it back to earth.

(18) Some NASA officials involved in the project admits privately that this news couldn't come at a better time. (19) Over the last decade, at least three major missions to Mars has failed at huge cost to the taxpayers. (20) A billion dollars are an enormous amount of cash to spend without anything to show for it.

CHAPTER 11 – TEST A   FORMING BASIC TENSES FOR REGULAR VERBS

Circle the verb in parentheses that correctly completes the sentence.

1. Roberta already (belong, belongs) to a health club.

2. Once of the boxes in the attic (need, needs) to be moved to the office.

3. The coach and the fans (believe, believes) the team deserves the award.

4. A student who (study, studies) regularly will probably pass his courses.

5. The gardeners who work for the community college always (plant, plants) zinnias in the bed by the main drive.

6. Each of my brothers (live, lives) in New York City.

Rewrite each of the following sentences two ways: using the past tense, and then using the future tense.

7. My silk blouse wrinkles in the washing machine.

Past: _____

Future: _____

8. The spaghetti tastes terrible.

Past: _____

Future: _____

9. My dad loves that movie.

Past: _____

Future: _____

Fill in the blank with the correct form of the verb in parentheses. The sense of the sentence requires the simple past tense or one of the perfect tense forms.

10. Sylvia (play) _____ _____ tennis for

years before she finally (decide) _____ to try racquetball.

11. Tourists (visit) _____ _____ that

museum daily for sixteen years now.

12. Mr. Schultz (interview) _____ three people before he finally

(select) _____ one for the job.

13. Molly (delay) _____ _____ her

wedding for one year.

14. I (ask) _____ _____ for a raise two times, but my

boss (refuse) _____ _____ my request each time.

CHAPTER 11 – TEST B   FORMING BASIC TENSES FOR REGULAR VERBS

Fill in each blank with the indicated tense of the verb in parentheses.

(1) The morning coffee on which many people (depend--present) _____

to start each day has a long history. (2) Coffee drinking first (start--past)_____

in Africa. (3) In fact, the name of the bean (trace--present) _____ back to

the name of its native province, Caffa. (4) Some details about the origin of coffee (remain--

present) _____ unknown, but it (seem--present) _____

that ancient Ethiopians may (discover--perfect) _____ the energizing effect

of coffee. (5) African storytellers (claim--present) _____ that a goatherd

named Kaldi (notice--past) _____ that his goats, instead of becoming

drowsy in the evenings, sometimes (play--past) _____ very actively until

very late. (6) Kaldi (realize--past) _____ that the goats (nibble--perfect)

_____ berries from a certain shrub. (7) He (wonder--past) _____

what was going on, so he (try--past) _____ some himself. (8) The

wakefulness and exhilaration that (result--past) _____ was so exciting that he

took some to the chief, who (decide--past) _____ to give the berries to the

villagers so they would stay awake during the long evening worship hours. (9) Today, coffee

still (help--present) _____ people stay awake.

(10) Today, gourmet shops (offer--present) _____ many special coffee

blends. (11) A coffeelover (choose--present) _____ from African, South

American, or Asian types. (12) In the future, even more specialized coffee varieties (develop--

future) _____. (13) Coffee certainly (continue--future) _____

to get folks going in the morning.

CHAPTER 12 – TEST A   USING IRREGULAR VERBS CORRECTLY

Circle the verb in parentheses that correctly completes the sentence.

1. My cousin and his wife (is, are) shopping for a new car.

2. Many visitors to Mexico (take, takes) courses in Spanish before traveling.

3. Either of those applicants (has, have) the qualifications to do the job.

4. Where (does, do) the directions say we should lay the foundation?

5. Those of us who (eat, eats) a nourishing breakfast are healthier because of it.

6. One of the desserts (is, are) enough for my sister and me to share.

Rewrite each of the following sentences two ways: first, using the past tense, then using the future tense.

7. The camera is in the suitcase.

Past: _____

Future: _____

8. Our neighbors grow broccoli in their garden.

Past: _____

Future: _____

9. Ruth drives to the cabin to take care of the yard.

Past: _____

Future: _____

Fill in each blank with the correct form of the verb in parentheses. The sense of the sentence requires the simple past tense or one of the perfect tenses.

10. My son Kalijah (do) _____ _____ his homework
    at the dining room table ever since he started school.

11. _____ you (see) _____ the Seinfeld show about Kramer's first name?

12. The Holts (give) _____ just _____ their old car to Goodwill Industries.

13. That woman (run) _____ _____ for the school board four times, but she _____ never (win) _____.

14. Last week, Yolanda, (drive) _____ to Idaho for her family reunion.

15. Jeffrey (write) _____ _____ several poems before he finally (choose) _____ one for the writing contest.

CHAPTER 12 – TEST B   USING IRREGULAR VERBS CORRECTLY

Fill in each blank with the indicated tense of the verb in parentheses.

(1) No other vegetable product (be--present) _____ as old as sugar.

(2) This sweetening agent (make--present) _____ food tasty and (give--present)

_____ foods the fuel to create energy. (3) Humans (know--perfect)

_____ about the oldest natural sugar, honey, ever since people first (see--past)

_____ bears raiding a bee hive. (4) Indeed, honey (become--past)

_____ so important that farmers domesticated bees and (put--past)

_____ them to work making honey fulltime. (5) Early scribes (write--perfect)

_____ in mythology a story about the origins of sugar. (6) The mother of the god

Zeus (hide--past) _____ her infant son in a cave so that his angry father could not

find him. (7) Bees (come--past) _____ along and (feed--past)

_____ him honey. (8) As a reward, Zeus (repay--past) _____ his

new friends with high intelligence and the ability to make sugar.

(9) Man's hunger for sugar (lead--perfect) _____ him to look for other sources

of sugar. (10) Throughout history, people (eat--perfect) _____ many different

plants mainly because of their sweetness. (11) Today, sugar cane and the sugar beet (take--

perfect) _____ the place of bees as the main sources of sugar. (12) Artificial

sweeteners (be--present) _____ popular among people who watch their diets

closely, and naturally sweet fruits (have--present) _____ an important place in a

healthy diet. (13) Anyone who (think--present) _____ that sugar isn't a mainstay

of the average American diet should take a closer look at ingredient labels the next time he or she

(make--present) _____ dinner or (drink--present) _____ a soda.

CHAPTER 13 – TEST A   PASSIVE VOICE, PROGRESSIVE TENSES, AND MAINTAINING CONSISTENCY IN TENSE

Underline the complete verb. In the blank identify its voice as either active or passive.

1. Our band was chosen to play at the festival.   _____

2. Tina's wedding dress is being sewn by her aunt.   _____

3. Mayor Smith had already called the meeting to order.   _____

4. A production of *Hamlet* will be presented at the college.   _____

In the space below, rewrite each sentence changing the verb to the passive voice.

5. Spike Lee directed the movie Do the Right Thing.

_____

6. Next week, the bank will sell the land.

_____

In the space below, rewrite each sentence changing the verb to the active voice.

7. I was fined $12 by the library for the overdue book.

_____

8. Every day, Jana is driven to school by her grandmother.

_____

Fill in the blank with the appropriate progressive tense of the verb in parentheses.

9. Phuong and Bill (plan) _____ a March wedding.

10. Marc (cook) _____ dinner for us tonight.

11. The wrestlers (stare) _____ at each other for an entire minute when the match finally started.

12. My son (sleep) _____ in the hammock outside.

13. We (have) _____ fun until the rain started.

14. You can't speak to Becky now; she (study) _____.

15. We (look) _____ for the car keys when we suddenly remembered where they were.

Revise the following sentences to make the verbs consistent. Cross out any errors. Write the correct tense above the line.

16. Luisa first worked in marketing for a large company; then she starts her own advertising firm.

17. Just when we were convinced we were lost, a troop of girl scouts comes hiking up the trail toward us.

18. When we travel to Rhode Island, we drove up Route 1 to enjoy the scenery.

19. Fred runs into the kitchen yelling and grabbed the fire extinguisher.

20. Last night we were watching television when all of a sudden a tree falls through the roof.

CHAPTER 13 – TEST B   PASSIVE VOICE, PROGRESSIVE TENSES, AND MAINTAINING CONSISTENCY IN TENSE

Proofread the following paragraph. Revise the underlined verbs, or the sections containing verbs, as necessary to correct errors in voice, progressive tense, and consistency in tense. Cross out any errors and write your additions or corrections above the lines. If an underlined verb form is correct, write C above it.

(1) There is much that <u>can learned</u> from ancient cultures. (2) In his book, *A Path with Heart*, Jack Kornfield tells the story of a tribe in East Africa where a strong sense of community <u>helped</u> a person grow up close to family and fellow villagers. (3) This connection begins even before a child <u>born.</u> (4) In fact, the birth date of a person <u>counted</u> from the first moment the mother dreams of her unborn son or daughter. (5) While the mother thinks of her intended child and the intended father, <u>a song is heard in her heart by her.</u> (6) She sits alone under a tree and <u>listened</u> for the song of the child she <u>hoping</u> to conceive. (7) <u>The song is sung to her heart by the Great Spirit.</u> (8) When the song <u>came</u>, the mother <u>goes</u> to teach it to the intended father. (9) They <u>singing</u> it together while the child is conceived. (10) While she is pregnant, she continually <u>singing</u> this special, individual song to the child in her womb. (11) She teaches it to the midwives so that they <u>singing</u> it to the child even as it <u>born.</u> (12) The child <u>greeted</u> into this world with his or her own song. (13) The song <u>continued</u> with the person throughout life. (14) It <u>sung</u> whenever the child falls and hurts itself or <u>needed</u> support during difficult times. (15) Also, in times of initiation or passage, the villagers celebrate with the song. (16) It is part of the wedding ceremony when the person <u>married.</u> (17) Even at the end of life, the loved ones gather around the deathbed and <u>sang</u> the song for the last time.

CHAPTER 14 – TEST A   ADDITIONAL ELEMENTS OF VERB USE

Circle the helping verb in parentheses that correctly completes each sentence.

1. Nobody I know (can, could) hike thirty miles in one day.

2. Roger wishes that he (can, could) juggle five balls at a time.

3. On the night of the storm, we (can, could) not find any flashlights, so we had to use the old oil lamp.

4. Grandfather is quite sure that he (can, could) pass his driving test.

5. If you were so brave, why (can't, couldn't) you go into the dark cave?

6. The people sitting behind you (can't, couldn't) see the stage if you stand there.

7. Everyone in our class assumed that Mary (will, would) one day be a doctor.

8. Bobbie says that dinner (will, would) be ready in half an hour.

9. Since we wanted to see Washington, DC, we decided we (will, would) leave a few days early.

10. Ellie says that it (will, would) be fine with her if we stay.

11. Ed said that it (will, would) be a disaster if we left.

12. No one knows when the next meteor shower (will, would) come.

Fill in each blank with the correct form of the verb <u>to be</u>.

13. Deb _____ too tired to wash the pots and pans last night, so she left them in the sink.

14. I can see that you _____ confused; let me explain it again.

15. For the past year, we _____ _____ looking for a house to buy.

16. By tomorrow night, Frank _____ _____ ready for the concert.

17. Ms. O'Malley _____ the best teacher they have at that school.

18. The kids _____ impolite to my guests yesterday.

19. Iris _____ _____ very sad until her husband came back from his business trip.

20. Folk dancing _____ my favorite weekend pastime, so I try to go often.

CHAPTER 14 – TEST B   ADDITIONAL ELEMENTS OF VERB USE

In each blank, write the form of the verb <u>to be</u> that correctly completes the sentence.

(1) The next time you must speak in front of a group, remember that public speaking _____ the number one fear for most people. (2) In fact, people _____ more afraid of giving a speech than they _____ of dying. (3) The fear of speaking _____ _____ a reality for students in introductory speech classes since time immemorial, but it _____ also a problem for actors and businesspeople. (4) Anyone who has ever had nervousness before giving a speech _____ probably familiar with the physical symptoms. (5) Some of these _____ tenseness in the throat, sweaty palms, and high blood pressure. (6) Understanding what anxiety really _____ can _____ a major step to overcoming the problem. (7) Anxiety _____ actually a surge of nervous energy that can really _____ used to your advantage. (8) A speaker might _____ nervous over the power to control the audience, so he or she might use that power to prepare thoroughly. (9) Instead of _____ nervous and using up all your energy, practice the speech ahead of time. (10) While you _____ speaking, look for a friendly face, and focus your energy on some visual aids.

Circle the helping verb in parentheses that correctly completes the verb phrase in each sentence.

(11) Most beginning college students (will, would) experience another kind of communication anxiety. (12) This is listening anxiety, and if you are not aware of it, it (can, could) get in the way of fully comprehending what you hear in class lectures. (13) There are two kinds of listening that often (will, would) compete inside your head: listening to others and listening to your own inner thoughts. (14) Especially if you are wishing you (can, could) be somewhere else, listening can be difficult and therefore an anxiety problem. (15) Actually, the normal person (can, could) barely listen for more than seven or eight minutes without a break. (16) If you can train yourself to monitor your attention when it begins to stray, then perhaps you (will, would) never again miss major parts of lessons in your classes.

CHAPTER 15 – TEST A   USING NOUNS AND PRONOUNS

Circle the noun in parentheses that correctly completes each sentence.

1. Many of the (man, men) attending the council meeting wore suits.

2. Jake and Sally already subscribe to one of the (magazine, magazines) their son was selling for school.

3. The bus driver counted each (child, children).

4. Both (parent, parents) need to be at the teacher conference.

5. Either of those picture (frame, frames) will make a nice gift.

Write the plural form for each noun in the blank.

6. shelf   _____

7. tooth   _____

8. mother-in-law   _____

9. fish   _____

Circle the pronoun in parentheses that correctly completes each sentence.

10. Dan brought snacks for Stella and (I, me) this morning.

11. "Jeff and (I, me) need a new playhouse," begged Travis.

12. Bob and (she, her) were at the movies until 11:30 last night.

13. Carrie knows that she can type better than (he, him).

14. The clerk forgot to give Andy and (I, me) a receipt.

15. Rick's parents say that he eats as much as (they, them) do.

16. The usher took Corrine and (she, her) to the wrong seats.

17. The Millers and (they, them) are going on a vacation together.

In each sentence, circle the pronoun that needs to be changed, omitted, or clarified.

18. On the news they said that crime is increasing.

19. Lisa wrote to Jane while she was on vacation.

20. My brother he is a mechanic who specializes in diesel engines.

CHAPTER 15 – TEST B   USING NOUNS AND PRONOUNS

Proofread the following passage for errors in noun use. Cross out each incorrect form and write the correct one above the line.

(1) Several recent Disney studio movie have introduced classic stories and historical figures to a generation. (2) One of the American woman made popular through such a movie is Pocahontas. (3) However, Hollywood's version is not entirely a factual accounts. (4) One fact that differs from the movie version is that Pocahontas was only twelve year old when she saved the life of John Smith. (5) Her actions were likely part of one of the traditional adoption ceremony of her people. (6) Pocahontas was not involved romantically with John Smith, although her kindness and intervention improved the lifes of the Jamestown colonists.

As the passage continues, circle the pronoun in parentheses that correctly completes each sentence.

(7) The colonists were indeed indebted to Pocahontas since (they, them) and Chief Powatan were not on the best of terms. (8) No one did more than (she, her) to make the relations better. (9) Pocahontas admired Smith and gave (he, him) and the colonists food; she also warned them of her father's plans for violence. (10) The highly regarded Pocahontas was persuaded to come on board ship where the English temporarily held (she, her) captive. (11) Her captors and (she, her) spent some time during which she converted to Christianity, fell in love, and married widower John Rolfe. (12) Pocahontas and (he, him) went to England in 1616 with an entourage of about a dozen Indians. (13) There the leaders introduced (they, them) to the royal court and held Pocahontas up as an example of how the native savages could be civilized. (14) Pocahontas, whose name had been changed to Rebecca, died before ever returning home and is buried in England, but today we celebrate (she, her) as the first American heroine.

In the last part of the passage, proofread for errors in plurals and pronouns. Cross out the errors and write the correct answers above the line. If a sentence is correct, write C above it.

(15) There is another lesser known Native American heroine whom made several significant contribution during the westward expansion period of American history. (16) Born in 1787, Sacagawea was sold to a French Canadian man who became her husband. (17) Because she spoke Shoshone, her and her husband were chosen to translate for Lewis and Clark. (18) An extraordinary feats was her rescue of all their supplys when the boat capsized. (19) She also saved the explorers from starvation by her knowledge of native foods and they preparation.

(20) Early colonization and westward expansion in America owe much to these two brave woman.

CHAPTER 16 – TEST A   MAINTAINING PRONOUN-ANTECEDENT AGREEMENT

Fill in each blank with the pronoun form that correctly completes the sentence.

1. The tennis players are trying to improve _____ serves.

2. Anybody who wants a job should submit _____ application here.

3. The committee has elected _____ new chairperson.

4. Each instructor in the department has _____ own office.

5. This new car needs to have _____ windshield cleaned.

6. People who do not always think before _____ speak.

7. One of my best friends married _____ childhood boyfriend.

8. These are the colors for my new kitchen. Do you like _____?

9. One of the candidates for mayor asked _____ wife to speak for him.

10. The band will play _____ next concert a week from Friday.

11. The teams will display _____ trophies in the school lobby.

12. Has someone wiped _____ dirty hands on my new tablecloth?

Add a logical second sentence to each sentence below. Begin your sentence with the demonstrative pronoun in parentheses.

13. When I was in high school, I lost a very special ring by leaving it at the bowling alley.

(This) _____

14. There are two important qualities I look for in a new friend.

(These) _____

Circle the verb in parentheses that agrees with the antecedent of the relative pronoun.

15. I dislike a doctor who (is, are) arrogant and condescending to patients.

16. The plant workers, who (was, were) on break, were watching TV.

17. A pen that (leak, leaks) can really ruin a dress shirt.

18. One of my aunts, who (live, lives) in Hawaii, has invited me to visit.

Revise each sentence to avoid sexist language by changing the antecedent.

19. Each of the dentists has his own waiting room.

_____

20. Anyone with a question should raise his hand.

_____

CHAPTER 16 – TEST B   MAINTAINING PRONOUN-ANTECEDENT AGREEMENT

In the paragraphs below, circle the word in parentheses that correctly completes each sentence.

(1) The African-American struggle for civil rights in (this, that) country shows us how the courageous actions of individuals can lead to major change. (2) The earliest achievements that (was, were) made for civil rights came from (these, those) in government just after the Civil War; however, in recent decades private individuals have fueled the movement.

(3) Modern protest activity got (its, their) start in Montgomery, Alabama, from Rosa Parks. (4) On December 1, 1955, Ms. Parks refused to give up (her, their) seat near the front of a city bus to a white rider. (5) (This, These) simple but brave defiance resulted in a boycott of the city buses when she was jailed. (6) Emerging from the boycott was an outstanding leader, Martin Luther King, Jr.; anyone who (know, knows) anything about American life in this century is aware of King's leadership. (7) A year after the Montgomery bus boycott, his exceptional skills in speaking and leading others had (its, their) reward when the buses were finally desegregated. (8) Dr. King continued to speak out for nonviolent protest, which he thought (was, were) the best tool for social change. (9) In August, 1963, his famous speech, with (its, their) theme "I Have a Dream," inspired a nation.

(10) (This, That) 1963 speech marked what was actually the second protest march planned for Washington. (11) The first one, which (was, were) planned for 1941, never actually took place. (12) However, (its, their) organizer, a dynamic leader named Philip Randolph, may have been the model for Dr. King. (13) (He, Randolph), president of the Brotherhood of Sleeping Car Porters, called for a protest march when discrimination stopped blacks from being hired for defense jobs in the early 1940s. (14) Randolph canceled the march when President Roosevelt issued (his, their) order to end the discrimination.

(15) Another small group of individuals left (its, their) imprint on the civil rights movement. (16) On February 1, 1960, four young college students in Greensboro, North Carolina, held a sit-in, refusing to give up (his, their) seats at a Woolworth lunch counter until (them, they) were served. (17) This unyielding team sat for days, and (it, they) inspired students all over the South.

(18) The African-American civil rights movement has left (its, their) mark on our democracy. (19) Other groups, such as women, gays, and the elderly, have followed the example of nonviolent protest in (its, their) struggles to gain rights. (20) Individuals can truly make a difference, not only in (his/her, their) own lives, but also in the life of a nation.

CHAPTER 17 – TEST A   USING MODIFIERS

Circle the modifier in parentheses that will correctly complete each sentence.

1. I can move very (quick, quickly) when I need to.

2. Steve told Jean that his love would remain (constant, constantly) through the years.

3. Caleb is very (creative, creatively) in his stained glass work.

4. He annoyed everyone by talking (loud, loudly) during the movie.

5. The broker promised to call her client (real, really) soon.

6. It was a (good, well) basketball game that went into double overtime.

7. Marcia yelled so much during the game that she did not feel (good, well) after it was over.

8. Brooke paints extremely (good, well), but she doesn't discipline herself.

9. Jack has an (awful, awfully) cold, so he'll stay in bed today.

10. Ned (energetic, energetically) cleaned up the whole house today.

11. The (worse, worst) part of the summer camp was kitchen duty.

12. Delia is usually (less, least) demanding than her twin sister.

Fill in each blank with the comparative or superlative form of the modifier in parentheses in order to correctly complete the sentence.

13. The computer will soon be _____(easy) to use than the telephone.

14. Yours is the _____ (low) of the five estimates we received.

15. Of the two semifinalist poems, I think yours is the _____ (good).

16. The _____ (wet) spring I can remember was in 1992.

17. This cold is even _____ (bad) than the one I had last year.

18. Ms. Simms is the _____ (recent) addition to the library staff.

Correct the double negative problems in these sentences. Cross out the error and write the correction above the line.

19. Ted couldn't see no point in staying on the fishing pier past midnight.

20. Hasn't nobody called back to return the message?

CHAPTER 17 – TEST B   USING MODIFIERS

In the paragraphs below, circle the modifier that correctly completes each sentence.

(1) My friend Paul is a (real, really) cautious person who usually doesn't take risks (easy, easily). (2) The (more, most) adventurous thing he has ever done was spend a year in England after he finished community college. (3) He (original, originally) went to visit a cousin stationed there, but he ended up working at a conference center for almost a year. (4) To this day, Paul appreciates the (many, more, most) things he learned and experienced during that year.

(5) Even though the British language and culture is similar to America's, Paul soon realized that he was indeed in a different country. (6) For one thing, the weather there was much (damp, damper, dampest) than in his native Arizona. (7) (Sudden, Suddenly) rain showers were an almost daily occurrence. (8) The winter he spent was the (worse, worst) he could imagine, with the wet cold penetrating his bones. (9) Still, he had to admit he didn't mind the wet weather because England also had the (more, most) beautiful gardens he had ever seen. (10) It seemed to him that even the (tiny, tinier, tiniest) yard was full of color. (11) Paul became quite a (well, good) gardener through his volunteer work in the conference center's garden. (12) His (previous, previously) training in horticulture was (certain, certainly) put to use.

(13) Another difference Paul noticed (quick, quickly) was the vocabulary used by his English friends. (14) He (eventual, eventually) began to use words such as "Cheerio" and "bloke." (15) He learned that it was (better, best) to ask the waiter for a "serviette" than for a "napkin" since "nappy" in England refers to a baby's diaper. (16) In a car, one checks the oil under the "bonnet" and puts suitcases in the "boot."

(17) Paul's year in England passed (rapid, rapidly). (18) He (final, finally) returned home because he missed his girlfriend so (bad, badly). (19) Nonetheless, he will always remember this adventure with (fond, fondest) memories.

CHAPTER 18 – TEST A   CAPITALIZING CORRECTLY

Proofread each sentence below for errors in capitalization. Cross out any errors and write the words correctly above the line.

1. The hurricane had done damage to much of the property at myrtle beach.

2. How many books have you and your friend susie read this summer?

3. I plan to sell these greek pastries at the bazaar next saturday.

4. During the korean war, american troops fought under the command of general MacArthur.

5. On thanksgiving day, our family will eat dinner at uncle gene's house.

6. Two of the courses i wanted to take, typing and german, have been canceled.

7. The bombing of the world trade center in new york was an act of terrorism.

8. When I took scott to washington, we loved the lincoln memorial at dusk.

9. My grandma's favorite meal consists of maine lobster and steamed asparagus.

10. Driving southwest across the nevada desert, we were thirsty for gatorade.

11. The neighborhood known as adams morgan features ethnic diversity; there's even an ethiopian restaurant.

12. Hannah's cousin plays her own songs every year at the lone star music festival in austin, texas.

13. The senator will speak to the rotary club while on her campaign trip through the south.

14. Did you happen to see the bulls game last night?

15. My uncle teaches several speech classes; his favorite is interpersonal communication 162.

16. Shelly's new dog is a maltese, named after an island called malta, which is in the mediterranean sea.

17. The treaty of ghent ended the war of 1812 between the united states and great britain.

18. After high school, Tiffany attended gallaudet university for one year.

19. Newer headache medications such as advil and aleve are quite popular.

20. Anyone studying to become a doctor will probably study chemistry and latin.

CHAPTER 18 – TEST B   CAPITALIZING CORRECTLY

Proofread the paragraphs below for errors in capitalization. Cross out any errors and write the words correctly above the lines.

(1) My best friend from childhood has a somewhat unusual job for a woman; she's a Truck driver. (2) Although husband and wife teams are becoming more common, Bonnie drives alone for north American van lines, a company based in fort wayne, indiana. (3) She's been doing this since the days when Truck Stops didn't even offer showers for women. (4) She would either have to ask some other driver to guard the shower or get a room at a days inn or other motel.

(5) Bonnie got started in her traveling career after her favorite cousin took her in his rig to west point military academy. (6) They delivered twelve xerox machines to the offices of the School over one labor day weekend, and she was hooked. (7) Bonnie didn't learn at a certified truck driving school such as new england tractor-trailer academy but on the job as an assistant to a veteran driver. (8) She's well suited to the job because she doesn't mind physical labor, and she's very skilled at dealing with customers as well as her Dispatcher.

(9) What she likes best, though, is being able to see the Country. (10) She has traveled through forty-five of the states and has often spent extra time in an area. (11) Her favorite destination is the west coast. (12) When she gets a load going westward, she packs her antique schwinn bicycle in the trailer so she can ride along the pacific after her delivery. (13) Bonnie has learned a great deal of inside information about her job site, america. (14) She knows where to find all the best truck stops, restaurants, backroad short cuts, and Shopping Centers.

(15) As one might imagine, she has collected a lot of great stories to tell her family when she comes home every christmas. (16) There's the tale of the freak spring snowstorm on the donner pass in northern california. (17) Once, she delivered a 2000 year old chinese screen to an art

gallery in new york. (18) Among the interesting people she's met are the former prime minister of england and one of mae west's boyfriends. (19) Of course, she has been met with lots of surprised looks at loading docks in Companies across the land. (20) Once they see the quality of her work, however, they have to agree with Bonnie when she says, "being a woman doesn't keep me from doing my job!"

CHAPTER 19 – TEST A   USING PUNCTUATION PROPERLY

Proofread the following sentences for proper punctuation. You may need to add periods, question marks, exclamation points, colons, semicolons, quotation marks, or apostrophes. Insert punctuation as needed above the lines.

1. You must bring several items to the exam clean paper, a sharpened pencil, and a dictionary

2. That mans wife asked us if we knew how to change a flat tire

3. The diver had trained for months he placed third in the Olympic trials

4. Help shouted the frightened child at the top of the sliding board

5. Is that your car rolling down the hill with its lights on

6. The artists best work was never seen during his lifetime

7. Which movie do you want to go see said Sarah to her little brother

8. If I could invite anyone to dinner, Id invite only two people Bill Clinton and Mother Teresa

9. Oh, by the way, said Jeremy, have you ever seen me juggle

10. There at the meeting sat Chuck Brown, the lawyer Janet Tobias, the accountant and Chris Wiley, the chairman of the company

11. The cat is lying there with its paws crossed around a pencil What a cute thing

12. Whos teaching your stained glass workshop asked Dave

13. A weeks vacation may not be enough to get me completely rested

14. Theres not enough sugar in the coffee for Ollie add another spoonful

15. George questioned his final grade in the course

16. Langston Hughes poem called Dream Deferred begins with a question

17. Nora ran to get help meanwhile we moved away from the smoking car

18. Did the weatherman say when its supposed to rain

19. Im going off to bed said the old man

20. All the golfers clubs were left in the rain four bags of clubs were ruined

CHAPTER 19 – TEST B   USING PUNCTUATION PROPERLY

Proofread the following paragraphs for proper punctuation. Insert periods, questions marks, exclamation points, colons, semicolons, quotation marks, or apostrophes as needed above the lines. If a sentence is correct, write C above it.

(1) If you were born into a home where English was spoken to you in your early years, you learned our languages idioms along with its vocabulary without having to study (2) Idioms are expressions that have a special meaning beyond the literal meanings of their words they carry a message different from the meanings of the individual words (3) For example, consider what it means when someone says to you, Give me a hand (4) How can you give someone else a hand (5) The native speaker knows that this means to help the person in some way. (6) There are plenty of other examples under the weather, scratch the surface, frame of mind, to get cold feet. (7) All of these are expressions that will bring a puzzled look to some students faces (8) When youre in a conversation with a friend who speaks English as a second language, watch for that puzzled look furthermore, watch your own conversation to see how common idioms really are

(9) Some other potential confusion for speakers of English as a second language can come from a words multiple meanings (10) For example, how many different meanings can you think of for the word pick (11) There are a lot of things a pick can be a sharp tool used to break up ground, a plastic tool used to play a guitar, or a kind of comb used to groom curly hair (12) A salesperson might say Take your pick or We prosecute pickpockets (13) A mothers advice might include telling her child not to pick at his or her food or not to pick a fight (14) Do you see how these different uses might confuse a new speaker of English (15) Think about other words that have several meanings and idiomatic uses call, put, or take are just a few (16) Try your best to explain what these sentences mean

(17) Dont bite my head off

(18) Shes a woman after my own heart

(19) He was getting in the teachers hair

(20) Idioms and various word meanings really make our language interesting and colorful we just have to be sensitive to our friends who may need a little explanation.

CHAPTER 20 – TEST A   USING COMMAS

Insert commas above the lines as needed in the following sentences.

1. Unless we get some rain soon the vegetable garden will dry up.

2. Felicia's twin daughters were born on September 30 1991.

3. Giovanni's an excellent Italian restaurant is moving to a new location.

4. We will need to prepare salad sandwiches and birthday cake for the picnic.

5. Driving slowly down the icy road we counted twelve minor accidents.

6. A pet can be a loving companion but it can also be a big responsibility.

7. She could not as a matter of fact remember her old boyfriend's name.

8. They lived in Nome Alaska before moving to Tampa Florida.

9. Her high school softball coach who had become a dear friend was retiring.

10. Tell me again Grandpa about your experiences in the Great Depression.

11. Edna whispered "I'll be back in a minute."

12. Leaning too far back in her seat Kelly tipped over and fell on the floor.

13. Oxford a city in central England is best known for its university.

14. After he had finished writing his paper Pedro took a nap.

15. "I'm sick and tired of tuna for dinner" moaned Terry.

16. On Saturdays Sue works in the yard goes to the pool and visits her dad.

17. I can't forget Tuesday May 7 1989 when my house burned down.

18. Louis Armstrong also known as "Satchmo" was a jazz trumpeter and singer.

19. I will not I repeat give you permission to borrow my car.

20. Ordinarily I watch Jeopardy after dinner.

CHAPTER 20 – TEST B   USING COMMAS

Proofread the following paragraphs for missing commas. Insert commas above the lines as needed.

(1) Cathie a friend of mine from church really enjoys her work once a month with our local soup kitchen. (2) She has been volunteering there since August 1991 on the first Sunday of every month. (3) Cathie believes in the importance of helping the less fortunate and she feels good about putting this belief into action. (4) Besides the good feeling she gets from helping others she appreciates the friendships and sense of teamwork that have developed from working with the same people over time. (5) She feels as a matter of fact that she gets as much out of the endeavor as do those they serve.

(6) Every month she is one of the first to arrive and begin setting out chairs making coffee or wrapping utensils in napkins. (7) After most of the team of workers has arrived they have a brief meeting to discuss the day's menu and assign jobs. (8) The meal which is always well balanced is planned the day before by a staff dietitian. (9) Menus are based on the food on hand which is sometimes donated from area restaurants or grocery stores. (10) The captain of the first Sunday team who has been with the group for twenty years is very skilled at supervising the process. (11) While some cooks begin to cut vegetables or open cans others set up the table with salt pepper and any other condiment the particular meal calls for. (12) Someone cuts up cakes or pies for dessert and another volunteer prepares the beverage station. (13) During the preparation time one of Cathie's regular duties is to count out plates. (14) They know how many plates they start with and later they count the ones that are left to discover how many people have been served. (15) On a typical Sunday they serve around three hundred homeless people. (16) Of course this is a small number compared to that of a city like Washington DC or

Los Angeles California but it's a considerable number for a small Midwestern city like ours.

(17) Cathie's team members try to treat the visitors as they would guests who are eating in their own homes. (18) They welcome diners guide them four at a time to seats and then bring the prepared plates to the table. (19) Trying to maintain eye contact they graciously say "You're quite welcome" when thanked. (20) Cathie along with everyone on her team ends up feeling like a true member of the family of humanity.

CHAPTER 21 – TEST A   MASTERING SPELLING

In the space provided, write the word created by combining the prefix or suffix and the root word as indicated.

1. un + natural = _____

2. bear + able = _____

3. study + ing = _____

4. forget + ing = _____

5. re + read = _____

6. commit + ment = _____

7. manage + able = _____

8. lonely + er = _____

Circle the correctly spelled word in each pair.

9. breif   /   brief

10. judgement   /   judgment

11. achieve   /   acheive

12. radioes   /   radios

13. sufficient   /   sufficeint

Circle the word that correctly completes each sentence.

14. What (affect, effect) will this rain have on your picnic plans?

15. The band members will march (past, passed) the principal's box seat.

16. Stan's (conscious, conscience) never bothers him, no matter what he does.

17. Paula and Rico's new car is parked over (their, there).

18. Izzy cannot remember (were, where) she left her notebook.

19. (Your, You're) welcome in our house any time.

20. I do not feel that I ought to (except, accept) that money.

CHAPTER 21 – TEST B   MASTERING SPELLING

In the blanks, supply the missing words by putting together the parts given in parentheses.

(1) Over the past few decades, there has been a growing (commit + ment) _____ to taking care of our earth. (2) Even young children are (worry + ing) _____ these days about protecting the environment. (3) Much has (occur + ed) _____ to help each of us know how to help. (4) Books such as *Fifty Simple Things You Can Do to Save the Earth* show us how to make environmental protection a part of our (day + ly) _____ lives. (5) None of us can close up the hole in the ozone layer, but all of us can make it our (busy + ness) _____ to stop using the chlorofluorocarbons (CFCs) that worsen the ozone problem. (6) Each of us is (response + ible) _____.

(7) One thing that many families already do is (re + cycle) _____. (8) Many communities have programs that provide convenient containers, which makes saving newspaper or glass quite (manage + able) _____. (9) To save water, never leave the tap (run + ing) _____ when you wash dishes or brush your teeth. (10) Picking up trash as you find it in the neighborhood sets a good example and makes your surroundings more (beauty + ful) _____.

Cross out each misspelled word and write the word correctly above the line.

(11) The things your able to do around your home are not only easy but also economical. (12) Saving energy saves money, and it might also save frustration to make your home less clutterred. (13) One way to do this is to stop recieving so much junk mail. (14) To do this, write to Mail Preference Service; its address is Direct Marketing Association, 11 West 42nd Street, PO Box 3861, New York, NY 10163-3861. (15) Another way to reduce paper is too use your own cloth or string bag when you shop. (16) That way, when the clerk asks, "Paper or plastic?" you can reply, "Niether!" (17) Their are certain kinds of packaging you should avoid completely, such as foam. (18) Its easy to save alot of water when flushing the toilet by placing a

plastic bottle in the tank to displace some of the water the tank will hold. (19) Taking care of our planet is everyone's job. (20) Anyone whose not part of the solution is part of the problem.

CHAPTER 22 – TEST A   MAINTAINING PARALLELISM

In each group, circle the part that is not parallel with the rest.

1. Chinese eggrolls
    bread from France
    Greek salad
    Mexican tacos

2. to go home
    to the bank
    to the drycleaners
    to the drug store

3. who was ready
    who was prepared
    who was patient
    who had an air of confidence

4. cute
    funny
    with wealth
    tall

In the sentences below, fill in each blank with a word or phrase that will maintain parallel structure in the sentence.

5. My hobbies include hunting, fishing, and _____.

6. Janet usually wants to go out on weekends while her husband _____
    _____.

7. You look very _____ and _____ today.

8. At the gift shop, we bought Dad a book and _____.

9. To get to the cabin from here, go across the field and _____.

10. Her motto is "Look good, act tough, and _____."

11. Attend class, sit up front, and _____ if you want to succeed in college.

12. Uncle Jed's old truck shook, sputtered, and _____.

Change words or phrases to make the following sentences parallel. Cross out errors, and write your corrections above the lines.

13. In the oath of office, the President swears to preserve, protect, and to defend the Constitution of the United States.

14. My vacation this summer had all the best ingredients: beautiful view, great companionship, and the weather was sunny.

15. Whoever gets this job will have to be conscientious, friendly, and with a sense of responsibility.

16. From the window she could see the corn fields, the barn that was old, and the distant hills were in view too.

17. Luke is a student, a businessman, and he has two kids.

18. By driving all night, eating in the car and we only stopped to fill up with gas, we were able to reach Detroit by noon.

19. Arnold Arboretum is a good place for a walk or to teach kids about trees.

20. Carol has decided to be either a nurse or she might like to teach school.

CHAPTER 22 – TEST B   MAINTAINING PARALLELISM

Proofread the following paragraphs for parallel structure. Cross out any errors, and write the corrections above the lines as needed. For sentences 12 and 17, write in the blanks sentence beginnings that will be parallel to the sentence beginning of the second paragraph (sentence 5).

(1) America's diverse mixture of ethnic backgrounds and communities has caused the country to be called a melting pot or a bowl with salad in it. (2) Just as our population is quite varied, our language also contains a wide range of varying word uses, word origins, and expressions that are regional. (3) Learning the stories behind word origins can help a student learn new vocabulary and remembering new vocabulary is easier too. (4) Besides, it can be fun to learn about words or trying out new words in conversations.

(5) One way our language adds new words is to borrow from other languages. (6) Many of the individual words that appear in an American dictionary originated in foreign languages. (7) In addition to these, we are beginning to borrow more and more conversational expressions from other languages. (8) For example, most of us know how to say and we have the understanding of the word "goodbye" in several languages. (9) "Adios" is Spanish, "ciao" is Italian, and "Cheerio" comes from Britain. (10) We say "Bon voyage!" when someone leaves for a trip or "Eureka!" is what we can say when we find or realize something. (11) We might describe a friend as having "chutzpah," which is Yiddish, or as having "wanderlust," which comes from the German.

(12) Another _____ to borrow from science or technology. (13) Many of these new words are acronyms, which are formed from the first letters of a title or string of words. (14) Reading the newspaper, listening to the radio, or when we watch TV, we might encounter words such as "NATO" or "SALT." (15) Everyone knows what a "yuppie" or a "zip" code is even though the words they come from may not be as

familiar. (16) Those who study computers or working in the computer field know abut "DOS"

and "RAM."

(17) Still _____ to borrow

from literature or legend. (18) For example, a myth tells of a man in Hades who was tortured by

the gods. (19) He was forced to stand in a pool of cool water that disappeared whenever he bent

to drink; overhead were branches of wonderful fruit blowing out of reach with him trying to eat.

(20) His name was Tantalus, and this is where we get the word "tantalize."

MASTERY TEST

Circle the letter of the choice that best completes the sentence or gives a correct statement about the sentence.

Section 1: Subject and Verbs, Fragments, Subordination, Coordination, Run-ons, and Comma Splices

1. The cataloging of books in this library is presently being converted to the computer system.
   - A. subject = books   &   verb = is being
   - B. subject = cataloging   &   verb = is being converted
   - C. subject = library   &   verb = is being converted

2. One of the exercise bicycles needs a new seat.
   - A. subject = one   &   verb = needs
   - B. subject = exercise   &   verb = needs
   - C. subject = bicycles   &   verb = needs

3. An understanding of world history will help students in many ways.
   - A. subject = history   &   verb = help
   - B. subject = history   &   verb = will help
   - C. subject = understanding &   verb = will help

4. Ken's car had been thoroughly inspected and tuned up before the trip.
   - A. subject = Ken's   &   verb = had been inspected
   - B. subject = car   &   verb = had been thoroughly inspected
   - C. subject = car   &   verb = had been inspected, tuned

5. It saddened her greatly.
   - A. The group of words is a sentence.
   - B. The group of words is not a sentence.

6. Dan so astonished that he couldn't speak to anyone at the surprise party.
   - A. The group of words is a sentence.
   - B. The group of words is not a sentence.

7. Trying to catch a glimpse of the movie stars in the restaurant, he walked backwards.
   - A. The group of words is a sentence.
   - B. The group of words is not a sentence.

8. While I was at home waiting for the plumber to come repair the sink.
   - A. The group of words is a sentence.
   - B. The group of words is not a sentence.

9. Hannah wasn't allowed to go to the _____ she had lied to her mom.
   A. beach, because
   B. beach although
   C. beach because

10. _____ Jose moved to Maine, he had never seen the ocean.
    A. Unless
    B. Until
    C. While

11. Hannah enrolled in _____ her daughter said she was too old.
    A. college although
    B. college, although
    C. college; although

12. Vimla wanted to be a _____ she changed her major from music to foods.
    A. chef and
    B. chef so
    C. chef, so

13. At first I was just _____ I became angry.
    A. upset, then
    B. upset, and then
    C. upset and then

14. Andrew proposed to her in _____ was very romantic.
    A. Paris; it
    B. Paris since
    C. Paris and

15. "I'm just about ready, make yourself at home," said Debbie.
    A. The sentence is correct.
    B. There is a problem that needs correcting.

16. The dog was barking loudly as if he had seen a stranger.
    A. The sentence is correct.
    B. There is a problem that needs correcting.

17. The food ran out before the party was _____ we had to order pizza.
    A. over, we
    B. over we
    C. over; we

Section 2: Verbs, Voice, Tenses, and Consistency

18. Mark cracks his knuckles all the _____ irritates his girlfriend.
    A. time this
    B. time, and this
    C. time, this

19. One of my neighbors _____ his lawn every day all day long.
    A. water
    B. waters
    C. watered

20. I think Mom and Dad _____ the anniversary party we are planning.
    A. will enjoy
    B. enjoy
    C. are enjoying

21. By working overtime last month, the club members _____ enough money to give the coach a nice gift at his retirement party.
    A. saving
    B. will save
    C. had saved

22. Have you _____ much money to charities this year?
    A. gave
    B. given

23. Hilda feels that her husband _____ far too much on her birthday gift.
    A. has spended
    B. have spent
    C. has spent

24. When I saw the ice cream truck go by, I _____ after it.
    A. ran
    B. run
    C. will run

25. At the lake last summer, my kids _____ several interesting rocks.
    A. finding
    B. found
    C. find

26. Chuck _____ his lunch every day, but he never _____ it.
      A. brings . . . ate
      B. brings . . . eats
      C. has brought . . . ate

27. Jackson and Sons Contracting Company built our new house.
      A. This sentence has a verb in the active voice.
      B. This sentence has a verb in the passive voice.

28. When the phone rang, I _____ into the shower.
      A. stepped
      B. am stepping
      C. was stepping

29. Vickie says that she _____ give me a ride to the airport next Wednesday.
      A. would
      B. will
      C. could

30. The clowns _____ silly, and their antics are making the children laugh.
      A. were
      B. will be
      C. are being

Section 3: Nouns, Pronouns, and Modifiers

31. The bank's telephone system allows you to transfer money between _____.
      A. account
      B. accounts

32. My grandmother has given most of her china to my sister and _____.
      A. me
      B. I
      C. myself

33. Sonia is a good dancer, but Carlos can dance better than _____ can.
      A. her
      B. hers
      C. she

34. Chris and _____ are going to the business meeting together.
      A. I
      B. me
      C. us

35. Somebody forgot to clean up _____ own mess.
    A. his or her
    B. their
    C. our

36. Everyone was stunned when the jury returned _____ verdict.
    A. their
    B. its

37. Cigarettes are hazardous to your health and expensive. _____ are two reasons to try to quit smoking.
    A. That
    B. This
    C. These

38. Books that _____ well worn and well read usually stand the test of time.
    A. is
    B. are

39. Michael washes dishes _____ than anyone else in our family.
    A. most careful
    B. most carefully
    C. more carefully

40. The reason Irina is such a _____ administrator is that she listens _____.
    A. good . . . well
    B. good . . . good
    C. well . . . good

41. Marta was the _____ person I ever roomed with, and she was the _____ cook, too!
    A. most messy . . . worst
    B. messiest . . . worse
    C. messiest . . . worst

42. The Underwood family _____ ends meet since their home burned; our church is helping them.
    A. can hardly make
    B. can't hardly make

Section 4: Punctuation, Capitals, Spelling and Parallel Structure

43. While Owen was driving _____, he had two flat tires.
    A. south to Stone Mountain
    B. South to Stone Mountain
    C. south to Stone mountain

44. Hugo was so angry that he threatened to write a letter to _____.
    A. governor Whitman
    B. Governor Whitman

45. For _____ Walter gave his _____ a hammock.
    A. Fathers' day . . . dad
    B. Fathers' Day . . . dad
    C. Fathers' Day . . . Dad

46. The _____ had been stolen from their unlocked trucks, so they all had to buy new ones.
    A. carpenter's tools
    B. carpenters tools'
    C. carpenters' tools

47. "Where is my favorite _____ scowled Mr. Bostwick.
    A. pen?"
    B. pen"?
    C. pen,"

48. The committee is made up of representatives from four _____ Hillsdale, Gillespie, and Deerfield.
    A. towns, Conway,
    B. towns; Conway,
    C. towns: Conway,

49. _____ screamed Ed as his wife drove off with his only house key.
    A. "Wait,"
    B. "Wait!"
    C. "Wait"!

50. Teaching her son to fix his own _____ learned a few things herself about patience.
    A. breakfast Fran
    B. breakfast, Fran
    C. breakfast; Fran

51. Ernie's grandfather remembers _____ the happiest day of his life.
     A. April 17, 1956, as
     B. April 17, 1956 as
     C. April, 17, 1956,

52. The sequoia tree resists damage from _____ and lives to be very old and large.
     A. fungus, insects and fire
     B. fungus, insects, and fire,
     C. fungus, insects, and fire

53. The Willamette River, which flows north through Corvallis and _____ the Columbia near Portland.
     A. Albany, joins
     B. Albany joins
     C. Albany; joins

54. The _____ are cooking fast; please add some more water to the pan.
     A. potatoes
     B. potatos

55. Next month, the Wongs will be _____ back to a family reunion in Idaho.
     A. traveling
     B. travelling

56. Most people feel it is rude to criticize a person for his or her _____.
     A. believes
     B. beleifs
     C. beliefs

57. _____ willing to go _____ or not we take the air-conditioned van?
     A. Whose . . . weather
     B. Whose . . . whether
     C. Who's . . . whether

58. His hobby of collecting antique cars is harmless but _____.
     A. the expense is great
     B. expensive
     C. it takes a lot of money

59. Being chairperson of our committee will require your time, your energy, and _____.
     A. commitment
     B. your commitment
     C. the ability to be committed

60. She understands what needs to be done but not _____.

    A. how to do it

    B. knowing how it should be done

    C. the way to do it

DIAGNOSTIC TEST

Circle the letter of the choice that best completes the sentence or gives a correct statement about the sentence.

SECTION 1: SUBJECTS AND VERBS, SENTENCE FRAGMENTS, COORDINATION, SUBORDINATION, RUN-ON SENTENCES, AND COMMA SPLICES

1. Several of my mother's coworkers are planning a surprise birthday party for her.
   - A. subject = coworkers & verb = planning
   - B. subject = coworkers & verb = are planning
   - C. subject = several & verb = are planning

2. Have you read the article in today's paper about the possibility of life on Mars?
   - A. subject = life & verb = have read
   - B. subject = you & verb = have read
   - C. subject = article & verb = read

3. At early Quaker meetings, the men and women sat on opposite sides of the room.
   - A. subject = Quaker meetings & verb = sat
   - B. subject = men, & verb = sat
   - C. subject = men, women & verb = sat

4. Joan thought about the problem but had no idea how to solve it.
   - A. subject = Joan & verb = thought, had
   - B. subject = Joan & verb = thought
   - C. subject = problem & verb = had thought

5. Until I was twelve and discovered that I could depend on myself.
   - A. The group of words is a sentence.
   - B. The group of words is not a sentence.

6. The canary escaped.
   - A. The group of words is a sentence.
   - B. The group of words is not a sentence.

7. Hoping to catch a few bass with his new rod and reel.
   - A. The group of words is a sentence.
   - B. The group of words is not a sentence.

8. The vase broken before it was even out of the shopping bag.
   - A. The group of words is a sentence.
   - B. The group of words is not a sentence.

9. _____ the game was played, the umpire flipped a coin to see which team would bat first.
   A. Then
   B. Once
   C. Before

10. Although it was _____ took the kids to the zoo.
    A. raining, we
    B. raining we
    C. raining. We

11. Harold won't buy the _____ asks him to do so.
    A. tickets, unless his dad
    B. tickets. Unless his dad
    C. tickets unless his dad

12. We hung up the beautifully framed _____ the wall still looked bare.
    A. print, and
    B. print, but
    C. print, so

13. They watched the show in different _____ they had just had a big fight.
    A. rooms, since
    B. rooms for
    C. rooms, for

14. Steve and Janet went _____ went out to eat.
    A. shopping, and then they
    B. shopping, then they
    C. shopping and then they

15. At first everyone was nervous, we relaxed when the teacher told a joke.
    A. The sentence is correct.
    B. There is a problem that needs correcting.

16. The players felt grateful to the coach despite the fact that they had lost the game.
    A. The sentence is correct.
    B. There is a problem that needs correcting.

17. Molly's daughter was away at summer _____ house seemed lonely.
    A. camp, the
    B. camp, and the
    C. camp, then the

18. Frankie puts the empty ice cream carton back in the _____ really gets on my nerves.
    A. freezer it
    B. freezer, it
    C. freezer; it

SECTION 2: VERBS, VOICE, TENSES, AND CONSISTENCY

19. Most of my children's friends _____ the same school they do.
    A. attend
    B. attends
    C. has attended

20. At the next meeting, the committee _____ the fundraiser party.
    A. plan
    B. will plan
    C. planned

21. Wendy _____ all through the movie.
    A. cried
    B. cry
    C. will cried

22. Each of Nettie's children _____ one course at the arts center every summer.
    A. taken
    B. take
    C. takes

23. _____ the crew leader of the morning shift of carpenters arrived?
    A. Did
    B. Have
    C. Has

24. By last night, we had _____ them at the mall five times this week.
    A. saw
    B. seen
    C. seeing

25. Your son has not _____ all his lunch, and he wants dessert.
    A. eaten
    B. ate
    C. eat

26. The savings account money was all spent on the new refrigerator.
      A. This sentence has a verb in the active voice.
      (B.) This sentence has a verb in the passive voice.

27. When Fred called last night, Amy _____ a cake for his birthday.
      A. is baking
      (B.) was baking
      C. baked

28. All of a sudden her dad comes in and _____, "Fire!"
      A. yelled
      B. yelling
      (C.) yells

29. I _____ get to sleep last night because I was worried about my son.
      (A.) couldn't
      B. can't
      C. won't

30. The actors _____ already learning the lines before rehearsals started.
      A. have been
      (B.) were
      C. been

SECTION 3: NOUNS, PRONOUNS, AND MODIFIERS

31. My kids will not eat either of those _____ of cereal.
      A. kind
      (B.) kinds

32. Mom called after the departing bus, "Write to your father and _____!"
      A. I
      B. we
      (C.) me

33. The teacher has asked Kevin and _____ to be partners on the project.
      A. he
      (B.) him
      C. them

34. Did you know that Oliver and _____ are buying a small boat?
      A. me
      B. us
      (C.) I

35. The major airlines have reduced _____ fares to New York for the winter.
        A. its
        (B.) their
        C. our

36. Each of the women gymnasts _____ own gold medal.
        A. have   their
        B. has   their
        (C.) has   her

37. It has rained five days this week. _____ makes it difficult to keep up the lawn.
        (A.) This
        B. That
        C. These

38. I get impatient with people who _____ always late.
        A. is
        (B.) are
        C. were

39. Sandy says that Van Gogh's *Starry Night* is the _____ painting she has ever seen.
        A. beautifulest
        (B.) most beautiful
        C. more beautiful

40. Corey's mother trains horses so _____ that people from all over Oklahoma hire her.
        (A.) well
        B. good
        C. better

41. This cold is _____ than the one I had at this same time last year.
        A. worst
        B. bad
        (C.) worse

42. Vinnie can't _____ remember to take his medicine.
        (A.) ever
        B. hardly
        C. never

SECTION 4: CAPITALS, PUNCTUATION, SPELLING, AND PARALLEL STRUCTURE

43. Gus works at a _____ station at the edge of the _____.
      Ⓐ Texaco . . . Mojave Desert
      B. Texaco . . . mojave desert
      C. texaco . . . Mojave desert

44. Melanie's _____ has written a book that will soon be made into a movie.
      A. Uncle
      Ⓑ uncle

45. Jeremy wants to take _____ this semester.
      A. golf, psychology, and spanish
      B. Golf, Psychology, and Spanish
      Ⓒ golf, psychology, and Spanish

46. "Stop _____ yelled one twin as the other hit him with the wooden spoon.
      A. it,"
      B. it"!
      Ⓒ it!"

47. Leslie asked me if I would take her with me when I go to the _____
      Ⓐ store.
      B. store?

48. My mom's cafeteria has three _____ cake, chicken pie, and lasagna.
      A. specialties; carrot
      Ⓑ specialties: carrot
      C. specialties carrot

49. The _____ faces were worth over a million dollars each.
      A. model's
      Ⓑ models'
      C. models

50. While Tom was at the gym working _____ borrowed his car.
      A. out; Nancy
      B. out Nancy
      Ⓒ out, Nancy

51. In Deadwood, South _____ lost their traveler's checks.
      A. Dakota they
      Ⓑ Dakota, they

52. Their house, a ninety-five year old log _____ been renovated.
        A. cabin, has
        B. cabin has
        C. cabin – has

53. Tonight at rehearsal he wants only those playing violins, _____ to stay late.
        A. violas, and cellos,
        B. violas and cellos
        C. violas, and cellos

54. Both _____ of the pizza have mushrooms.
        A. halfs
        B. halves

55. Aren't you _____ something very important?
        A. forgetting
        B. forgeting

56. This store will give you a dollar if the clerk neglects to give you a _____.
        A. receipt
        B. reciept

57. _____ is no way _____ car will be ready in time for you to pick it up today.
        A. Their . . . your
        B. There . . . you're
        C. There . . . your

58. In his retirement, my father plans to keep a garden, to build a deck, and _____.
        A. lots of cooking out on the grill
        B. to cook meals out on the grill
        C. grilling food

59. With little money, few materials, and _____, Georgia was still able to build a model of her invention.
        A. almost no encouragement
        B. nobody to encourage her
        C. doing it without encouragement from others

60. Ahmed is a responsible employee, a sensitive husband, and _____.
        A. he loves his children
        B. one whose children are loved
        C. a loving father

DIAGNOSTIC TEST ITEM ANALYSIS

Test Items Missed				Chapter/Skill		#Correct/# on test
1	2	3	4	5	Subjects & Verbs	_____ / 4
5	6	7	8	6	Sentence Fragments	_____ / 4
9	10	11		7	Subordination	_____ / 3
12	13	14		8	Coordination	_____ / 3
15	16	17	18	9	Comma Splice & Run-On	_____ / 4
19	20	21		11	Regular Verbs	_____ / 3
22	23	24	25	12	Irregular Verbs	_____ / 4
26	27	28		13	Passive, Prog., Consistency	_____ / 3
29	30	31		14	Additional Verb Use	_____ / 3
32	33	34	35	15	Nouns & Pronouns	_____ / 4
36	37	38	39	16	Pronoun-Antecedent Agreement	_____ / 4
40	41	42		17	Modifiers	_____ / 3
43	44	45		18	Capitals	_____ / 3
46	47	48	49	19	Punctuation	_____ / 4
50	51	52	53	20	Commas	_____ / 4
54	55	56	57	21	Spelling	_____ / 4
58	59	60		22	Parallelism	_____ / 3

Total Correct = _____ / 60

CHAPTER 5 – TEST A   SUBJECTS AND VERBS

In each sentence circle the simple or compound subject and underline the verb or verb phrase.

1. The pink (clouds) in front of the sun <u>made</u> the sky beautiful.

2. (Uncle Walter) and his (wife) <u>have lived</u> in the Ozark Mountains all their lives.

3. The simple little (house) deep in the woods <u>was</u> a peaceful place to visit.

4. That (rascal) <u>hid</u> my bedroom slipper.

5. (Juan) and (Diane) <u>are</u> already <u>planning</u> a small wedding.

6. My (cousin) still <u>keeps</u> a bird sanctuary in her yard.

7. Nathan's first basketball (game) <u>will be played</u> tomorrow night.

8. Regular (exercise) <u>makes</u> me more energetic and <u>keeps</u> the excess pounds off.

9. The huge (increase) in the number of commuters <u>has caused</u> many traffic jams in our cities.

10. (Some) of the best chefs never <u>go</u> to formal cooking schools.

11. Her 1982 Toyota (wagon) <u>looks</u> like a wreck but <u>runs</u> well.

12. (Many) of the fans in the bleachers <u>have brought</u> binoculars.

13. By next summer, (I) <u>will have saved</u> enough money for a canoe.

14. The (cars) in the parking lot <u>are</u> too close together.

15. (Sam Nguyen) and his (brother) <u>have</u> just <u>opened</u> a new restaurant.

In the following sentences, circle the simple subject and underline the verb. In the blank to the right, identify the verb as an action verb (ACT) or a linking verb (LV).

16. (Tamara) <u>seems</u> angry about her daughter's decision.   LV

17. The golf (coach) and her star (player) <u>arrived</u> early.   ACT

18. On winter nights, a (fire) in the wood stove <u>feels</u> wonderful.   LV

19. The (stew) <u>tasted</u> too salty for most of the diners.   L V

20. Our (neighbors) across the street <u>have</u> a pool.   ACT

CHAPTER 5 – TEST B   SUBJECTS AND VERBS

In the paragraph below, circle the simple subject and underline the verb or verb phrase.

(1) (Most) of us <u>have heard</u> of women such as Clara Barton and Florence Nightingale. (2) These two (people) <u>made</u> great contributions to nursing education and earned reputations for themselves as pioneers. (3) Even young (students) frequently <u>recognize</u> the name of scientist Marie Curie. (4) (Rachel Carson,) a leader in environmental studies, <u>is</u> also <u>known</u> to a generation of Americans. (5) However, many other less famous (women) <u>have made</u> contributions to science and humanity. (6) For example, (Annie Jump Cannon) <u>was</u> a leading astronomer. (7) (She) <u>became</u> a Harvard professor in 1938. (8) (She) and several women (coworkers) <u>discovered</u> five thousand new stars. (9) The (work) of Lise Meitner in physics <u>played</u> an important part in the development of the atomic bomb. (10) Another (example) <u>is</u> Sonya Kovalesky, a Russian math professor. (11) (She) <u>studied</u> the movement of an object around a still point and <u>helped</u> with later work in the study of the stars. (12) Other unknown (women) <u>improved</u> the quality of people's lives. (13) (Julia Lathrop) <u>served</u> as the first chief of the Children's Bureau of the United States Department of Labor. (14) In the American West, (Nellie Cashman) <u>organized</u> relief efforts for miners with scurvy during the gold rushes of the 1870s. (15) An (organization) for the improvement of social conditions <u>was founded</u> by a woman, Margaret Slocum Sage. (16) (Many) of today's business management practices <u>can be traced</u> to Mary Parker Follett. (17) In the 1920s, (Mary Follett) <u>was</u> already <u>using</u> team management and cooperative conflict resolution. (18) (Some) of the women leaders in the areas of art and literature <u>might be</u> more familiar. (19) (Mary Cassatt) and (Georgia O'Keeffe) <u>have</u> certainly <u>added</u> to the beauty of our world. (20) Today, many (organizations) <u>celebrate</u> the achievements of great women and <u>educate</u> the public about their contributions.

CHAPTER 6 – TEST A   SENTENCE FRAGMENTS

Write S in the blank beside each complete sentence. Write F beside each fragment. In the space provided, rewrite each fragment as a complete sentence, adding or changing words as needed.
ANSWERS WILL VARY.

F   1. Climbing the crepe myrtles in their backyard.
We were climbing the crepe myrtles in their backyard.

S   2. Knowing the weeds in the flower bed had to be pulled, she got up early.

F   3. The Lewis and Clark expedition the first explorers in several of our western states.
The Lewis and Clark expedition were the first explorers in several of our western states.

F   4. Under the beach umbrella to avoid getting sunburned.
I sat under the beach umbrella to avoid getting sunburned.

F   5. While Jeff painted the ceiling and Mark fixed lunch.
While Jeff painted the ceiling and Mark fixed lunch, Jane took a nap.

S   6. It arrived in the mail yesterday.

F   7. To go white water rafting down the Colorado River.
My dream is to go white water rafting down the Colorado River.

S   8. Quilting was my great aunt's hobby and joy.

F   9. Outrageously overpriced in the specialty stores.
Those gadgets are outrageously overpriced in the specialty stores.

F   10. Rachel, a gifted organist who accompanies our choir.
Rachel, a gifted organist who accompanies our choir, is also a math teacher.

S   11. Listen to the eerie howl of that wind.

S   12. Kim, a young mother of twins and a full-time nurse, also volunteers for the Red Cross.

F   13. Until I can find a suitable babysitter.
Until I can find a suitable babysitter, I cannot plan to go.

F   14. Without even trying to repair the broken chair.
He left without even trying to repair the broken chair.

S   15. On the rug next to the fireplace lay a white cat.

For each of the following fragments, write in the blank what is needed to form a complete sentence. Label as follows:

    V   if it needs a verb
    HV   if it needs a helping verb
    S   if it needs a subject
    CI   if it needs a new complete idea

16. Wants to become a surgical technician.   S

17. The bowl broken into two large pieces.   HV

18. As Julio walked into the doctor's office.   CI

19. The last thing on her mind during the test.   V

20. Once upon a time in a country far away.   CI

CHAPTER 6 – TEST B   SENTENCE FRAGMENTS

Label each word group F if it is a fragment or S if it is a complete sentence. Then, revise this passage to correct each fragment. You can join them to other sentences or add words to make them into complete sentences. Be sure to use correct punctuation and capitalization. Write your corrections above the lines.

1. F   (1) One of the fondest memories I have of my childhood *is*

2. S   spending a week at Grandma's house in the country. (2) She lived on a

3. F   small farm *with* (3) ~~With~~ a big vegetable garden and an old rickety ~~barn~~ *barn, a*

4. F   (4) ~~A~~ reminder of the days when mules helped run the farm. (5)

5. F   Feeling like pioneer girls in the Old ~~West.~~ *West, my* (6). ~~My~~ sister and I ~~playing~~ *played*

6. F   for hours in the ancient wagon. (7) Working was also a major part of

7. S   any visit to Grandma's. (8) *We hoed* ~~Hoed~~ corn, shelled peas, and picked green

8. F   beans. (9) We explored the damp, dark ~~basement~~ *basement, where* (10) ~~Where~~ row

9. S   after row of canned vegetables and pickles stood, souvenirs of the past.

10. F   (11) *We took* ~~Taking~~ a break every morning to watch Grandma's favorite

11. F   "story" on television. (12) There was one daily chore that we fought for

12. S   the privilege of doing and usually ended up doing together. (13) *This was going* ~~Going~~

13. F   to the post office *which* (14) ~~Which~~ was actually located in a special

14. F   neighbor's house down the road. (15) Evenings spent on the porch,

15. S   hearing funny tales of my dad's childhood, were so special. (16) Time

16. S   flew. (17) Even as teenagers, my sister and I loved summer weeks on

17. S   Grandma's farm *although* (18) ~~Although~~ perhaps for different reasons. (19)

18. F   *We gained* ~~Gaining~~ a personal experience of my family's own history. (20) ~~A~~

19. F   *This remains a* precious gift in my adulthood.

20. F

CHAPTER 7 – TEST A   SUBORDINATION

Underline each main clause contained in the sentences below. Circle each subordinate clause. In the blank, write S if the sentence is simple or CX if the sentence is complex.

1. <u>Many visitors enjoy the mild weather in San Diego all year.</u>   S
2. (When it rains,) <u>the busy streets are full of umbrellas.</u>   CX
3. <u>You should never sign a contract</u> (until you have carefully read the fine print.)   CX
4. <u>Bill and Lindsay often go out to eat at the newest ethnic restaurants.</u>   S
5. <u>The woman</u> (that I called just now) <u>is a landscape architect.</u>   CX

Using the subordinating conjunction in parentheses, combine each of the following pairs of ideas. Punctuate the complex sentences correctly. Write your sentences on the lines provided.

6. Gene went to the checkout line.
    He had bought everything on his list.   (when)

Gene went to the checkout line when he had bought everything on his list.

7. You will not be allowed to go to the park.
    You finish your homework.   (until)

You will not be allowed to go to the park until you finish your homework.

8. I bought the jacket.
    I discovered it was ripped.   (after)

After I bought the jacket, I discovered it was ripped.

9. Marcy has taken so many days off.
    She is almost out of vacation time.   (since)

Since Marcy has taken so many days off, she is almost out of vacation time.

10. Everyone in the family is allergic to poison ivy.
    They all went walking in the dense woods.   (although)

Although everyone in the family is allergic to poison ivy, they all went walking in the dense woods.

Add either a subordinate clause or a complete idea to turn each word group into a logical complex sentence.

ANSWERS WILL VARY.

11. As Paula locked her office door, *she noticed the package in the hall*.

_____

12. I will be glad to type the report *if you give it to me soon*.

_____

13. The man *who bought the Taylor farm* is my uncle.

14. If I won the state lottery, *I would travel around the country*.

_____

15. I really like a book *that has interesting historical characters*.

_____

Where they are needed, insert commas in the sentences below. If a sentence does not need a comma, write C beside it.

16. Until their homework is finished, Sally and her brother aren't allowed to ride the horses.

17. My mother, who went to beauty college in Texas, now has a salon of her own.

18. Karla is working late again because the deadline is tomorrow.   C

19. The design that you turned in was chosen as first prize winner.   C

20. If the turtle is disturbed by noise or lights, she will not lay her eggs.

CHAPTER 7 – TEST B   SUBORDINATION

Underline each subordinate clause. If the sentence does not contain a subordinate clause, write S (for simple sentence) above it.

(1) A fun family vacation can involve a great deal of work. **[S]** (2) <u>Before the loaded-down minivan or car leaves home</u>, many decisions about the trip and arrangements must be made. (3) Deciding where to go in the first place isn't easy <u>if you have family members with different interests</u>. (4) One person might love the beach <u>while another person prefers to visit a city</u>. (5) **[S]** Those in charge of the planning must consider things such as weather, entertainment or educational opportunities, and budget. (6) Compromise and foresight are two essential elements of deciding the destination. (7) <u>After the place is determined</u>, the rest of the planning begins.

(8) A parent <u>who is in charge of arranging all the details</u> can be tired <u>before the trip even starts</u>.

Use an appropriate subordinating conjunction to join each of the following pairs of ideas into one sentence. Add subordinating conjunctions and commas as needed above the line. Change periods or capitals as needed.

(9) Most families with children take their vacations in the summer *while kids* ~~Kids~~ are out of school.

(10) Summer vacations might be a bit more difficult to plan *since roads* ~~Roads~~, hotels, campgrounds, and parks are busiest then. (11) Reservations *which can be made in advance* can help prevent disappointment and frustration. ~~Reservations can be made in advance~~. (12) *although planning* ~~Planning~~ details might sound like work *it* ~~It~~ can lay the foundation for a better time together. (13) *When a* ~~A~~ family is preparing a trip *it's* ~~It's~~ a good idea to let each person talk about what would make it fun.

Proofread each sentence for proper comma usage. Correct by adding commas as needed above the line.

(14) If family members enjoy very different activities**,** you should try to provide some of each kind of activity. (15) Travel agents**,** who can provide ideas about activities in a certain place**,** help

family members anticipate and plan for their time together. (16) A way to avoid

misunderstandings is to lay down a few general rules that will help everyone know what is

expected. (17) Share the meal or housekeeping duties while you are away from home. (18) If

you invest some time in careful planning, your vacation will be more pleasant as a result.

In the space below, write two complex sentences of your own about a vacation you have taken.
Make sure each sentence contains a subordinate clause.
ANSWERS WILL VARY.
19. _____

_____

20. _____

_____

CHAPTER 8 – TEST A   COORDINATION

Fill in each blank with a coordinating conjunction or a conjunctive adverb that makes sense. Read each sentence carefully for punctuation clues on which kind of word to insert.

ANSWERS MAY VARY-POSSIBLE ANSWERS NOTED

1. Most of the roads on the way were not paved, *so*　　　　Mike's car got very dirty.

2. They turned on the large window fan, *buy/yet*　　　　the room remained hot.

3. I may pack the car tonight, *or*　　　I may wait until tomorrow morning.

4. Sofia was visiting relatives in Mexico last month; *therefore/consequently*, she could not come to the party.

5. Maine is beautiful in the fall; *however, nonetheless*, it can be quite cold.

Combine each of the following pairs of sentences using coordinating conjunctions. Write your compound sentences on the lines below, being sure to use capitals and punctuation correctly.

6. The state's bridges must be repaired.
   Our highway infrastructure will be dangerous.

   The state's bridges must be repaired, or our highway infrastructure will be dangerous .

7. Roger has a large snowblower.
   His drive is always clean.

   Roger has a large snowblower, so his drive is always clean .

8. A volt is a unit of electrical power.
   An ohm is a unit of electrical resistance.

   A volt is a unit of electrical power, and an ohm is a unit of electrical resistance .

9. Women began to fight for the vote in the 1840's.
   They did not win that right until 1920.

   Women began to fight for the vote in the 1840's, but they did not win that right until 1920 .

10. Herb's favorite shoes are completely worn out.
    He walks miles in them everyday.

    Herb's favorite shoes are completely worn out, for he walks miles in them every day .

On the lines provided, add words to create compound sentences. Read each sentence carefully for clues to help you create logical sentences.

ANSWERS WILL VARY

11. Her neighbors keep their lights on all night, yet *they are seldom at home*

_____.

12. Lars bought the boat with his own money, so *he is taking good care of it.*

_____.

13. Taking a study skills class may help you manage your time; furthermore, *it can teach you*

how to study effectively _____.

Proofread these sentences for errors in the use of commas and semicolons. Insert the missing punctuation marks above the lines.

14. Butch's day-care job doesn't pay well; however, he loves working with the children.

15. The sunrise at Key West is beautiful, and the atmosphere is relaxed.

16. Her reply is clear; there can be no doubt about her feelings toward him.

17. My speedometer is not working properly, so I cannot tell how fast I am driving.

18. Howard Hughes was an extremely wealthy man, but was he happy?

19. It rained one day during our trip; otherwise, the weather was perfect.

20. I need a new job; I cannot stand the one I have.

CHAPTER 8 – TEST B   COORDINATION

Fill in each blank with a coordinating conjunction or a conjunctive adverb. Read each sentence carefully for punctuation clues on which type of word to use.
ANSWERS MAY VARY; SOME POSSIBLE ANSWERS NOTED

(1) Today there are over 200 known breeds of dogs, *but/and* all of these descended from only one animal, the wolf. (2) Dogs were first domesticated around 10,000 years ago; *therefore/hence*, there have been many generations for specific breeds to be created. (3) Some breeds were designed for certain looks or temperaments, *and* some were intended to do jobs around a home or farm. (4) Dogs could be workers, *or* they could be companions. (5) There are only six official classes of purebred dogs; *however*, there are thousands of mixtures possible.

Combine the following pairs of simple sentences with coordinating conjunctions. Insert commas and conjunctions above the line.

(6) Dogs of mixed breeds are officially called ~~mongrels. Those~~ *mongrels, but those* who love them call them pets. (7) Those who raise purebred dogs go to ~~shows. They~~ *shows, and they* can show their dogs and compete for prizes. (8) Paintings of dogs appear near those of people in ancient Egyptian ~~tombs. We~~ *tombs, so we* know that dogs were considered pets in those times.

Proofread the following sentences for errors in punctuation. Correct the sentences by inserting correct punctuation above the line.

(9) Dogs see the world differently than people do*;* objects look the same to them in darkness and in daylight. (10) Their hearing range is also very different*;* therefore*,* they can hear pitches that humans cannot hear. (11) Some breeds are especially intelligent*;* indeed*,* dogs have been trained to guide the blind or help quadriplegic patients. (12) Anyone who has loved a dog knows that dogs communicate with their body language*,* but a person has to know what certain signs mean. (13) A dog will wag its tail to show a friendly greeting*,* or it will go down on its

forepaws with its back end high to say, "Let's play!" (14) A beloved dog will help its owner relax; furthermore, studies show that a person's blood pressure actually lowers when talking to a pet. (15) At Christmas or on children's birthdays, many folks will adopt an adorable puppy; however, they should remember that puppies grow up to be dogs. (16) One should think seriously about the responsibilities of caring for a mature dog; otherwise, the cute puppy may wind up at a pound. (17) A dog can herd livestock for a rancher, or it can provide security to an elderly person who lives alone. (18) However, most people own dogs for a different reason; usually a person owns a dog to have a loyal friend.

On the lines below, write two compound sentences about any dog you have known. Make sure each of your sentences contains two complete ideas. Punctuate correctly.
ANSWERS WILL VARY.

19. _____

_____

20. _____

_____

CHAPTER 9 – TEST A   AVOIDING COMMA SPLICES AND RUN-ON SENTENCES

Proofread for errors in sentence combination. In the blank, write C beside a correct sentence, RO beside a run-on, or CS beside a comma splice.

RO   1. My college roommate Philip is now a playwright he lives and works in New York City.

CS   2. All the children in the day-care center take naps after lunch, it's the only quiet time of the day.

S   3. Keeping a journal is an effective way to overcome the anxiety that many new writers feel.

S   4. Before work, Sheila starts her day at the gym with a workout.

CS   5. Hang gliding began in California in the late 1960s, also known as sky surfing, it is most popular on the coast.

RO   6. Dag Hammarskjold won the Nobel Peace Prize in 1961 he was killed in a plane crash that year while on a trip for the United Nations.

CS   7. Shakespeare wrote plays about historical figures, for example, there really was a king of Scotland named MacBeth.

S   8. Frank and Trudie work in their garden every weekend, and all the neighbors enjoy their results.

RO   9. Katie's friend from Australia visited last year now she plans to go there for a few months.

S   10. Best known today as a poet, Wallace Stevens was also an insurance executive.

RO   11. Nancy will be playing her own music at the coffeehouse this is her first public appearance in our area.

CS   12. I cannot seem to find my keys, have you seen them?

Proofread for run-on sentences or comma splices. Correct errors using punctuation, coordination, or subordination. Write the corrected sentences on the lines provided. If the sentence is correct, write "Correct" on the line.
ANSWERS WILL VARY.

13. James will attend school to be an optician he has always wanted to help people see better.

_____

James will attend school to be an optician because he has always wanted to help people see better.

14. Pam's parents are moving to a nursing home, they can no longer take care of themselves.

_____

Pam's parents are moving to a nursing home, for they can no longer take care of themselves.

15. There were no seats left in the auditorium Don stood in the back to see the show.

_____

Since there were no seats left in the auditorium, Don stood in the back to see the show.

16. Hobbling along on her crutches, Tara tried to keep up with the others.

_____

Correct

17. New Orleans is a wonderful place to visit there is jazz music and great Creole cooking.

_____

New Orleans is a wonderful place to visit; there is jazz music and great Creole cooking.

Correct this run-on sentence three ways, according to the specific instructions below. Write each correction on the lines provided. Be sure to punctuate correctly.

Sam dyed his hair blue his parents are not too upset.

18. with a coordinating conjunction

_____

Sam dyed his hair blue, but his parents are not too upset.

19. with a semicolon

_____

Sam dyed his hair blue; his parents are not too upset.

20. with a subordinating conjunction

_____

Although Sam dyed his hair blue, his parents are not too upset.

CHAPTER 9 – TEST B   AVOIDING COMMA SPLICES AND RUN-ON SENTENCES

The following passage contains some run-ons and comma splices. Make corrections by adding conjunctions, punctuation, and capitalization as necessary above the line. Write C above each correct sentence.

ANSWERS MAY VARY.

(1) Have you ever wondered when some of our most common everyday items were ~~invented~~ *invented?* ~~you~~ *You* might be surprised to know how long some of these have been around. (2) Television has been around since ~~1926 a~~ *1926. A* color image was transmitted only three years later, in 1929. *C* (3) Our desk drawers contain some inventions from early this century. (4) Cellophane for tape originated in 1908, *and* paper clips date back to 1900. *C* (5) Carbon paper goes all the way back to 1806. (6) Some of the household tools we use have a long ~~history flashlights~~ *history. Flashlights* have shone since ~~1891 the~~ *1891, and the* electric hand drill was invented in 1895. (7) Although they weren't commonly used until much later, contact lenses were first created in 1887, *while* hearing aids date back to 1880. (8) *C* It may surprise you to learn that the use of microfilm, fluorescence, and the steam-powered airship all began in 1852. (9) Your track coach's stopwatch has been around since ~~1855~~ *1855;* your great grandmother's sewing machine might be an original 1846 model. (10) The next time you turn up the air conditioning with the thermostat or mow your yard, think of the year ~~1830 that's~~ *1830. That's* when these activities became possible. *C* (11) Scientists have known about he caffeine in your coffee since 1821 and the sodium in your potato chips since 1807. (12) Let's not overlook the flush ~~toilet, it~~ *toilet, which* was invented in 1778!

Write C in the blank beside each correct sentence. Write CS beside each comma splice or RO beside each run-on.

S   13. Other inventions might surprise you for a different reason.

CS   14. It may seem that some familiar devices have been around forever, they are actually inventions of the past few decades.

RO   15. DNA fingerprinting was first used in 1986 the megabit computer chip of 1984 is a relative newcomer.

RO   16. Most of us own CD players these have been around only since 1984, and the CD-ROM which we use on our computers is from 1985.

CS   17. We have heard of "test tube babies" for years, the first child developed from a frozen embryo was born in 1985.

S   18. Even while you are completing this test, inventors are developing products and processes that will soon be a part of our everyday lives.

Correct this run-on in two different ways. Write your sentences in the lines below.
ANSWERS WILL VARY.
Inventors improve our world we should give them credit.

19. *Inventors improve our world, so we should give them credit.*

20. *Inventors improve our world; we should give them credit.*

CHAPTER 10 – TEST A   SUBJECT-VERB AGREEMENT

Underline the subject and circle the correct verb in each of the sentences of the following passage.

(1) Sports (remains/remain) a dominant part of U.S. popular culture. (2) As they have for years, people from all walks of life (follows/follow) the progress of their favorite teams. (3) In most major U.S. cities, the home team (enjoys/enjoy) great support from the public. (4) Also, with the availability of cable and satellite systems today, everybody with a few extra dollars (has/have) the opportunity to see far more games than ever before.

(5) The sales figures for clothing bearing the logo of a professional team also (illustrate/illustrates) American's on-going love affair with sports. (6) There (is/are) a team jersey or hat in many wardrobes throughout the country. (7) Economics (doesn't/don't) lie; millions of people pay plenty just so they can wear items like their favorite stars.

(8) In addition, over the last decade, interest in sports memorabilia (has/have) continued to grow. (9) There (has/have) been many published accounts of individuals who became rich after finding a valuable baseball card at a yard sale somewhere. (10) (Doesn't/Don't) everyone today know the potential value of old baseball cards?

(11) National exposure provided by cable broadcasters like ESPN and MTV (has/have) produced a whole new generation of superstars: extreme athletes. (12) Today's new pros (doesn't/don't) hit homeruns or score goals. (13) For these athletes, a skateboard or a special bike (is/are) required equipment. (14) Both the X-Games and the Gravity Games (has/have) drawn the attention of millions to these extreme athletes.

(15) Anybody who thinks these people aren't athletes obviously (has/have) never watched them perform. (16) (Has/Have) these critics ever tried to ride straight up a ramp, do a flip in the

air, and continue riding? (17) <u>Strength and agility</u> (is/(are)) vital to these athletes, just as they are

for other top professionals. (18) An <u>event</u> such as street luge, with participants careening down

steep, winding hills, flat on their backs, on a platform slightly larger than a skateboard,

((calls)/call) for toughness and courage.

    (19) Clearly, <u>both traditional and extreme sports</u> (continues/(continue)) to hold the public's

interest. (20) Thanks to extensive media coverage, <u>fans</u> of both kinds of sports (has/(have)) plenty

of opportunity to cheer on their favorites.

CHAPTER 10 – TEST B   SUBJECT-VERB AGREEMENT

Each sentence in the following passage contains an error in subject-verb agreement. Correct the errors by crossing out the incorrect verb and writing the correct verb form above the incorrect one.

(1) NASA scientists studying Mars ~~has~~ *have* recently discovered evidence suggesting that water may exist on our neighboring planet. (2) The new theories about this vital fluid ~~is~~ *are* based on pictures transmitted by the Mars Global Surveyor. (3) The most recent images, up to 10 times sharper in focus than earlier pictures, ~~shows~~ *show* deep gullies and channels, evidence of water flowing.

(4) There ~~have~~ *has* long been speculation about the existence of water on Mars. (5) Even today, some people, like the early astronomers, ~~believes~~ *believe* the lines visible on the planet's surface are canals. (6) In more modern times, however, scientists ~~has~~ *have* proven that the idea of canals on Mars is science fiction, not science.

(7) Still, the various features of the Red Planet's landscape ~~continues~~ *continue* to inspire the idea of water at some past time. (8) The latest evidence ~~strengthen~~ *strengthens* these theories of water on Mars. (9) A key feature of the newest findings ~~are~~ *is* that the channels and gullies lack impact craters and other signs associated with millions of years of existence. (10) In fact, the gullies and channels in the recent photos ~~seems~~ *seem* relatively recent.

(11) Researchers studying the issue ~~argues~~ *argue* that water caused these geographical features. (12) But if there ~~are~~ *is* water, where is it? (13) The extreme temperatures on Mars ~~makes~~ *make* surface water impossible because it would either freeze or boil away. (14) Some experts therefore ~~believes~~ *believe* that the water lies beneath the surface of the planet.

(15) The prospect of water on Mars ~~excite~~ *excites* scientists because of the many implications and possibilities. (16) For example, the presence of subsurface water in sufficient

quantities ~~mean~~ *means* that life forms similar to forms on earth may have existed. (17) Also, in water there ~~are~~ *is* the essence of two potent rocket fuels, oxygen and hydrogen, so explorers would have what they need to make it back to earth.

(18) Some NASA officials involved in the project ~~admits~~ *admit* privately that this news couldn't come at a better time. (19) Over the last decade, at least three major missions to Mars ~~has~~ *have* failed at huge cost to the taxpayers. (20) A billion dollars ~~are~~ *is* an enormous amount of cash to spend without anything to show for it.

CHAPTER 11 – TEST A   FORMING BASIC TENSES FOR REGULAR VERBS

Circle the verb in parentheses that correctly completes the sentence.

1. Roberta already (belong, (belongs)) to a health club.

2. Once of the boxes in the attic (need, (needs)) to be moved to the office.

3. The coach and the fans ((believe,) believes) the team deserves the award.

4. A student who (study, (studies)) regularly will probably pass his courses.

5. The gardeners who work for the community college always ((plant,) plants) zinnias in the bed by the main drive.

6. Each of my brothers (live, (lives)) in New York City.

Rewrite each of the following sentences two ways: using the past tense, and then using the future tense.

7. My silk blouse wrinkles in the washing machine.

Past: _My silk blouse wrinkled in the washing machine._

Future: _My silk blouse will wrinkle in the washing machine._

8. The spaghetti tastes terrible.

Past: _The spaghetti tasted terrible._

Future: _The spaghetti will taste terrible._

9. My dad loves that movie.

Past: _My dad loved that movie._

Future: _My dad will love that movie._

Fill in the blank with the correct form of the verb in parentheses. The sense of the sentence requires the simple past tense or one of the perfect tense forms.

10. Sylvia (play) *had played* tennis for years before she finally (decide) *decided* to try racquetball.

11. Tourists (visit) *have visited* that museum daily for sixteen years now.

12. Mr. Schultz (interview) *interviewed* three people before he finally (select) *selected* one for the job.

13. Molly (delay) *has delayed* her wedding for one year.

14. I (ask) *have asked* for a raise two times, but my boss (refuse) *has refused* my request each time.

CHAPTER 11 – TEST B   FORMING BASIC TENSES FOR REGULAR VERBS

Fill in each blank with the indicated tense of the verb in parentheses.

(1) The morning coffee on which many people (depend--present) _depend_ to start each day has a long history. (2) Coffee drinking first (start--past) _started_ in Africa. (3) In fact, the name of the bean (trace--present) _traces_ back to the name of its native province, Caffa. (4) Some details about the origin of coffee (remain--present) _remain_ unknown, but it (seem--present) _seems_ that ancient Ethiopians may (discover--perfect) _have discovered_ the energizing effect of coffee. (5) African storytellers (claim--present) _claim_ that a goatherd named Kaldi (notice--past) _noticed_ that his goats, instead of becoming drowsy in the evenings, sometimes (play--past) _played_ very actively until very late. (6) Kaldi (realize--past) _realized_ that the goats (nibble--perfect) _had nibbled_ berries from a certain shrub. (7) He (wonder--past) _wondered_ what was going on, so he (try--past) _tried_ some himself. (8) The wakefulness and exhilaration that (result--past) _resulted_ was so exciting that he took some to the chief, who (decide--past) _decided_ to give the berries to the villagers so they would stay awake during the long evening worship hours. (9) Today, coffee still (help--present) _helps_ people stay awake.

(10) Today, gourmet shops (offer--present) _offer_ many special coffee blends. (11) A coffeelover (choose--present) _chooses_ from African, South American, or Asian types. (12) In the future, even more specialized coffee varieties (develop--future) _will develop_. (13) Coffee certainly (continue--future) _will continue_ to get folks going in the morning.

CHAPTER 12 – TEST A   USING IRREGULAR VERBS CORRECTLY

Circle the verb in parentheses that correctly completes the sentence.

1. My cousin and his wife (is, **are**) shopping for a new car.
2. Many visitors to Mexico (**take,** takes) courses in Spanish before traveling.
3. Either of those applicants (**has,** have) the qualifications to do the job.
4. Where (does, **do**) the directions say we should lay the foundation?
5. Those of us who (**eat,** eats) a nourishing breakfast are healthier because of it.
6. One of the desserts (**is,** are) enough for my sister and me to share.

Rewrite each of the following sentences two ways: first, using the past tense, then using the future tense.

7. The camera is in the suitcase.

Past: _The camera was in the suitcase._

Future: _The camera will be in the suitcase._

8. Our neighbors grow broccoli in their garden.

Past: _Our neighbors grew broccoli in their garden._

Future: _Our neighbors will grow broccoli in their garden._

9. Ruth drives to the cabin to take care of the yard.

Past: _Ruth drove to the cabin to take care of the yard._

Future: _Ruth will drive to the cabin to take care of the yard._

Fill in each blank with the correct form of the verb in parentheses. The sense of the sentence requires the simple past tense or one of the perfect tenses.

10. My son Kalijah (do) _has done_ his homework at the dining room table ever since he started school.

11. _Have_ you (see) _seen_ the Seinfeld show about Kramer's first name?

12. The Holts (give) *have* just *given* their old car to Goodwill Industries.

13. That woman (run) *has* *run* for the school board four times, but she *has* never (win) *won*.

14. Last week, Yolanda, (drive) *drove* to Idaho for her family reunion.

15. Jeffrey (write) *had* *written* several poems before he finally (choose) *chose* one for the writing contest.

CHAPTER 12 – TEST B   USING IRREGULAR VERBS CORRECTLY

Fill in each blank with the indicated tense of the verb in parentheses.

(1) No other vegetable product (be--present) *is* as old as sugar. (2) This sweetening agent (make--present) *makes* food tasty and (give--present) *gives* foods the fuel to create energy. (3) Humans (know--perfect) *have known* about the oldest natural sugar, honey, ever since people first (see--past) *saw* bears raiding a bee hive. (4) Indeed, honey (become--past) *became* so important that farmers domesticated bees and (put--past) *put* them to work making honey fulltime. (5) Early scribes (write--perfect) *have written* in mythology a story about the origins of sugar. (6) The mother of the god Zeus (hide--past) *hid* her infant son in a cave so that his angry father could not find him. (7) Bees (come--past) *came* along and (feed--past) *fed* him honey. (8) As a reward, Zeus (repay--past) *repaid* his new friends with high intelligence and the ability to make sugar.

(9) Man's hunger for sugar (lead--perfect) *has led* him to look for other sources of sugar. (10) Throughout history, people (eat--perfect) *have eaten* many different plants mainly because of their sweetness. (11) Today, sugar cane and the sugar beet (take--perfect) *have taken* the place of bees as the main sources of sugar. (12) Artificial sweeteners (be--present) *are* popular among people who watch their diets closely, and naturally sweet fruits (have--present) *have* an important place in a healthy diet. (13) Anyone who (think--present) *thinks* that sugar isn't a mainstay of the average American diet should take a closer look at ingredient labels the next time he or she (make--present) *makes* dinner or (drink--present) *drinks* a soda.

CHAPTER 13 – TEST A   PASSIVE VOICE, PROGRESSIVE TENSES, AND MAINTAINING CONSISTENCY IN TENSE

Underline the complete verb. In the blank identify its voice as either active or passive.

1. Our band <u>was chosen</u> to play at the festival.   *passive*

2. Tina's wedding dress <u>is being sewn</u> by her aunt.   *passive*

3. Mayor Smith had already <u>called</u> the meeting to order.   *active*

4. A production of *Hamlet* <u>will be presented</u> at the college.   *passive*

In the space below, rewrite each sentence changing the verb to the passive voice.

5. Spike Lee directed the movie <u>Do the Right Thing.</u>

The movie "Do The Right Thing" was directed by Spike Lee.

6. Next week, the bank will sell the land.

The land will be sold by the bank next week.

In the space below, rewrite each sentence changing the verb to the active voice.

7. I was fined $12 by the library for the overdue book.

The library fined me $12 for the overdue books.

8. Every day, Jana is driven to school by her grandmother.

Everyday, Jana's grandmother drives her to school.

Fill in the blank with the appropriate progressive tense of the verb in parentheses.

9. Phuong and Bill (plan) *are planning* a March wedding.

10. Marc (cook) *is cooking* dinner for us tonight.

11. The wrestlers (stare) *were staring* at each other for an entire minute when the match finally started.

12. My son (sleep) *is sleeping* in the hammock outside.

13. We (have) *were having* fun until the rain started.

14. You can't speak to Becky now; she (study) *is studying*.

15. We (look) *were looking* for the car keys when we suddenly remembered where they were.

Revise the following sentences to make the verbs consistent. Cross out any errors. Write the correct tense above the line.
SOME ANSWERS MAY VARY.

16. Luisa first worked in marketing for a large company; then she ~~starts~~ *started* her own advertising firm.

17. Just when we were convinced we were lost, a troop of girl scouts ~~comes~~ *came* hiking up the trail toward us.

18. When we travel to Rhode Island, we ~~drove~~ *drive* up Route 1 to enjoy the scenery.

19. Fred ~~runs~~ *ran* into the kitchen yelling and grabbed the fire extinguisher.

20. Last night we were watching television when all of a sudden a tree ~~falls~~ *fell* through the roof.

CHAPTER 13 – TEST B   PASSIVE VOICE, PROGRESSIVE TENSES, AND MAINTAINING CONSISTENCY IN TENSE

Proofread the following paragraph. Revise the underlined verbs, or the sections containing verbs, as necessary to correct errors in voice, progressive tense, and consistency in tense. Cross out any errors and write your additions or corrections above the lines. If an underlined verb form is correct, write C above it.

(1) There is much that can [be] learned from ancient cultures. (2) In his book, *A Path with Heart*, Jack Kornfield tells the story of a tribe in East Africa where a strong sense of community helped [helps] a person grow up close to family and fellow villagers. (3) This connection begins even before a child [is] born. (4) In fact, the birth date of a person [is] counted from the first moment the mother dreams of her unborn son or daughter. (5) While the mother thinks of her intended child and the intended father, ~~a song is heard in her heart by her.~~ [she hears a song in her heart] (6) She sits alone under a tree and listened [listens] for the song of the child she [is] hoping to conceive. (7) ~~The song is sung to her heart by the Great Spirit.~~ [The Great Spirit sings the song to her.] (8) When the song ~~came~~ [comes], the mother goes [C] to teach it to the intended father. (9) They [are] singing it together while the child is conceived. (10) While she is pregnant, she continually ~~singing~~ [sings] this special, individual song to the child in her womb. (11) She teaches it to the midwives so that they ~~singing~~ [can sing] it to the child even as it [is] born. (12) The child [is] greeted into this world with his or her own song. (13) The song ~~continued~~ [continues] with the person throughout life. (14) It ~~sung~~ [is sung] whenever the child falls and hurts itself or ~~needed~~ [needs] support during difficult times. (15) Also, in times of initiation or passage, the villagers celebrate with the song. (16) It is part of the wedding ceremony when the person ~~married~~ [marries]. (17) Even at the end of life, the loved ones gather around the deathbed and ~~sang~~ [sing] the song for the last time.

CHAPTER 14 – TEST A   ADDITIONAL ELEMENTS OF VERB USE

Circle the helping verb in parentheses that correctly completes each sentence.

1. Nobody I know (can, could) hike thirty miles in one day.

2. Roger wishes that he (can, could) juggle five balls at a time.

3. On the night of the storm, we (can, could) not find any flashlights, so we had to use the old oil lamp.

4. Grandfather is quite sure that he (can, could) pass his driving test.

5. If you were so brave, why (can't, couldn't) you go into the dark cave?

6. The people sitting behind you (can't, couldn't) see the stage if you stand there.

7. Everyone in our class assumed that Mary (will, would) one day be a doctor.

8. Bobbie says that dinner (will, would) be ready in half an hour.

9. Since we wanted to see Washington, DC, we decided we (will, would) leave a few days early.

10. Ellie says that it (will, would) be fine with her if we stay.

11. Ed said that it (will, would) be a disaster if we left.

12. No one knows when the next meteor shower (will, would) come.

Fill in each blank with the correct form of the verb to be.

13. Deb *was* too tired to wash the pots and pans last night, so she left them in the sink.

14. I can see that you *are* confused; let me explain it again.

15. For the past year, we *have* *been* looking for a house to buy.

16. By tomorrow night, Frank *will* *be* ready for the concert.

17. Ms. O'Malley *is* the best teacher they have at that school.

18. The kids *were* impolite to my guests yesterday.

19. Iris *had* *been* very sad until her husband came back from his business trip.

20. Folk dancing *is* my favorite weekend pastime, so I try to go often.

CHAPTER 14 – TEST B   ADDITIONAL ELEMENTS OF VERB USE

In each blank, write the form of the verb <u>to be</u> that correctly completes the sentence.

(1) The next time you must speak in front of a group, remember that public speaking <u>*is*</u> the number one fear for most people. (2) In fact, people <u>*are*</u> more afraid of giving a speech than they <u>*are*</u> of dying. (3) The fear of speaking <u>*has been*</u> a reality for students in introductory speech classes since time immemorial, but it <u>*is*</u> also a problem for actors and businesspeople. (4) Anyone who has ever had nervousness before giving a speech <u>*is*</u> probably familiar with the physical symptoms. (5) Some of these <u>*are*</u> tenseness in the throat, sweaty palms, and high blood pressure. (6) Understanding what anxiety really <u>*is*</u> can <u>*be*</u> a major step to overcoming the problem. (7) Anxiety <u>*is*</u> actually a surge of nervous energy that can really <u>*be*</u> used to your advantage. (8) A speaker might <u>*be*</u> nervous over the power to control the audience, so he or she might use that power to prepare thoroughly. (9) Instead of <u>*being*</u> nervous and using up all your energy, practice the speech ahead of time. (10) While you <u>*are*</u> speaking, look for a friendly face, and focus your energy on some visual aids.

Circle the helping verb in parentheses that correctly completes the verb phrase in each sentence.

(11) Most beginning college students (**will,** would) experience another kind of communication anxiety. (12) This is listening anxiety, and if you are not aware of it, it (**can,** could) get in the way of fully comprehending what you hear in class lectures. (13) There are two kinds of listening that often (**will,** would) compete inside your head: listening to others and listening to your own inner thoughts. (14) Especially if you are wishing you (can, **could**) be somewhere else, listening can be difficult and therefore an anxiety problem. (15) Actually, the normal person (**can,** could) barely listen for more than seven or eight minutes without a break. (16) If you can train yourself to monitor your attention when it begins to stray, then perhaps you (**will,** would) never again miss major parts of lessons in your classes.

CHAPTER 15 – TEST A   USING NOUNS AND PRONOUNS

Circle the noun in parentheses that correctly completes each sentence.

1. Many of the (man, **men**) attending the council meeting wore suits.

2. Jake and Sally already subscribe to one of the (magazine, **magazines**) their son was selling for school.

3. The bus driver counted each (**child**, children).

4. Both (parent, **parents**) need to be at the teacher conference.

5. Either of those picture (frame, **frames**) will make a nice gift.

Write the plural form for each noun in the blank.

6. shelf   *shelves*

7. tooth   *teeth*

8. mother-in-law   *mothers-in-law*

9. fish   *fish*

Circle the pronoun in parentheses that correctly completes each sentence.

10. Dan brought snacks for Stella and (I, **me**) this morning.

11. "Jeff and (**I**, me) need a new playhouse," begged Travis.

12. Bob and (**she**, her) were at the movies until 11:30 last night.

13. Carrie knows that she can type better than (**he**, him).

14. The clerk forgot to give Andy and (I, **me**) a receipt.

15. Rick's parents say that he eats as much as (**they**, them) do.

16. The usher took Corrine and (she, **her**) to the wrong seats.

17. The Millers and (**they**, them) are going on a vacation together.

In each sentence, circle the pronoun that needs to be changed, omitted, or clarified.

18. On the news (they) said that crime is increasing.

19. Lisa wrote to Jane while (she) was on vacation.

20. My brother (he) is a mechanic who specializes in diesel engines.

CHAPTER 15 – TEST B   USING NOUNS AND PRONOUNS

Proofread the following passage for errors in noun use. Cross out each incorrect form and write the correct one above the line.

(1) Several recent Disney studio ~~movie~~ *movies* have introduced classic stories and historical figures to a generation. (2) One of the American ~~woman~~ *women* made popular through such a movie is Pocahontas. (3) However, Hollywood's version is not entirely a factual ~~accounts~~ *account*. (4) One fact that differs from the movie version is that Pocahontas was only twelve ~~year~~ *years* old when she saved the life of John Smith. (5) Her actions were likely part of one of the traditional adoption ~~ceremony~~ *ceremonies* of her people. (6) Pocahontas was not involved romantically with John Smith, although her kindness and intervention improved the ~~lifes~~ *lives* of the Jamestown colonists.

As the passage continues, circle the pronoun in parentheses that correctly completes each sentence.

(7) The colonists were indeed indebted to Pocahontas since (they, them) and Chief Powatan were not on the best of terms. (8) No one did more than (she, her) to make the relations better. (9) Pocahontas admired Smith and gave (he, him) and the colonists food; she also warned them of her father's plans for violence. (10) The highly regarded Pocahontas was persuaded to come on board ship where the English temporarily held (she, her) captive. (11) Her captors and (she, her) spent some time during which she converted to Christianity, fell in love, and married widower John Rolfe. (12) Pocahontas and (he, him) went to England in 1616 with an entourage of about a dozen Indians. (13) There the leaders introduced (they, them) to the royal court and held Pocahontas up as an example of how the native savages could be civilized. (14) Pocahontas, whose name had been changed to Rebecca, died before ever returning home and is buried in England, but today we celebrate (she, her) as the first American heroine.

In the last part of the passage, proofread for errors in plurals and pronouns. Cross out the errors and write the correct answers above the line. If a sentence is correct, write C above it.

(15) There is another lesser known Native American heroine ~~whom~~ *who* made several significant ~~contribution~~ *contributions* during the westward expansion period of American history.

C

(16) Born in 1787, Sacagawea was sold to a French Canadian man who became her husband.

(17) Because she spoke Shoshone, ~~her~~ *she* and her husband were chosen to translate for Lewis and Clark. (18) An extraordinary ~~feats~~ *feat* was her rescue of all their ~~supplys~~ *supplies* when the boat capsized. (19) She also saved the explorers from starvation by her knowledge of native foods and ~~they~~ *their* preparation.

(20) Early colonization and westward expansion in America owe much to these two brave ~~woman~~ *women*.

CHAPTER 16 – TEST A   MAINTAINING PRONOUN-ANTECEDENT AGREEMENT

Fill in each blank with the pronoun form that correctly completes the sentence.

1. The tennis players are trying to improve *their* serves.

2. Anybody who wants a job should submit *his or her* application here.

3. The committee has elected *its* new chairperson.

4. Each instructor in the department has *his or her* own office.

5. This new car needs to have *its* windshield cleaned.

6. People who do not always think before *they* speak.

7. One of my best friends married *her* childhood boyfriend.

8. These are the colors for my new kitchen. Do you like *them*?

9. One of the candidates for mayor asked *his* wife to speak for him.

10. The band will play *its* next concert a week from Friday.

11. The teams will display *their* trophies in the school lobby.

12. Has someone wiped *his or her* dirty hands on my new tablecloth?

Add a logical second sentence to each sentence below. Begin your sentence with the demonstrative pronoun in parentheses.
ANSWERS WILL VARY.
13. When I was in high school, I lost a very special ring by leaving it at the bowling alley.

(This) *This really upset me.*

14. There are two important qualities I look for in a new friend.

(These) *These are dependability and sense of humor.*

Circle the verb in parentheses that agrees with the antecedent of the relative pronoun.

15. I dislike a doctor who (**is**, are) arrogant and condescending to patients.

16. The plant workers, who (was, **were**) on break, were watching TV.

17. A pen that (leak, **leaks**) can really ruin a dress shirt.

18. One of my aunts, who (live, **lives**) in Hawaii, has invited me to visit.

Revise each sentence to avoid sexist language by changing the antecedent.

19. Each of the dentists has his own waiting room.

The dentists have their own waiting rooms.

20. Anyone with a question should raise his hand.

Those with a question should raise their hands.

CHAPTER 16 – TEST B   MAINTAINING PRONOUN-ANTECEDENT AGREEMENT

In the paragraphs below, circle the word in parentheses that correctly completes each sentence.

(1) The African-American struggle for civil rights in (this, that) country shows us how the courageous actions of individuals can lead to major change. (2) The earliest achievements that (was, were) made for civil rights came from (these, those) in government just after the Civil War; however, in recent decades private individuals have fueled the movement.

(3) Modern protest activity got (its, their) start in Montgomery, Alabama, from Rosa Parks. (4) On December 1, 1955, Ms. Parks refused to give up (her, their) seat near the front of a city bus to a white rider. (5) (This, These) simple but brave defiance resulted in a boycott of the city buses when she was jailed. (6) Emerging from the boycott was an outstanding leader, Martin Luther King, Jr.; anyone who (know, knows) anything about American life in this century is aware of King's leadership. (7) A year after the Montgomery bus boycott, his exceptional skills in speaking and leading others had (its, their) reward when the buses were finally desegregated. (8) Dr. King continued to speak out for nonviolent protest, which he thought (was, were) the best tool for social change. (9) In August, 1963, his famous speech, with (its, their) theme "I Have a Dream," inspired a nation.

(10) (This, That) 1963 speech marked what was actually the second protest march planned for Washington. (11) The first one, which (was, were) planned for 1941, never actually took place. (12) However, (its, their) organizer, a dynamic leader named Philip Randolph, may have been the model for Dr. King. (13) (He, Randolph), president of the Brotherhood of Sleeping Car Porters, called for a protest march when discrimination stopped blacks from being hired for defense jobs in the early 1940s. (14) Randolph canceled the march when President Roosevelt issued (his, their) order to end the discrimination.

(15) Another small group of individuals left (its, their) imprint on the civil rights movement. (16) On February 1, 1960, four young college students in Greensboro, North Carolina, held a sit-in, refusing to give up (his, their) seats at a Woolworth lunch counter until (them, they) were served. (17) This unyielding team sat for days, and (it, they) inspired students all over the South.

(18) The African-American civil rights movement has left (its, their) mark on our democracy. (19) Other groups, such as women, gays, and the elderly, have followed the example of nonviolent protest in (its, their) struggles to gain rights. (20) Individuals can truly make a difference, not only in (his/her, their) own lives, but also in the life of a nation.

CHAPTER 17 – TEST A   USING MODIFIERS

Circle the modifier in parentheses that will correctly complete each sentence.

1. I can move very (quick, **quickly**) when I need to.

2. Steve told Jean that his love would remain (**constant,** constantly) through the years.

3. Caleb is very (**creative,** creatively) in his stained glass work.

4. He annoyed everyone by talking (loud, **loudly**) during the movie.

5. The broker promised to call her client (real, **really**) soon.

6. It was a (**good,** well) basketball game that went into double overtime.

7. Marcia yelled so much during the game that she did not feel (good, **well**) after it was over.

8. Brooke paints extremely (good, **well**), but she doesn't discipline herself.

9. Jack has an (**awful,** awfully) cold, so he'll stay in bed today.

10. Ned (energetic, **energetically**) cleaned up the whole house today.

11. The (worse, **worst**) part of the summer camp was kitchen duty.

12. Delia is usually (**less,** least) demanding than her twin sister.

Fill in each blank with the comparative or superlative form of the modifier in parentheses in order to correctly complete the sentence.

13. The computer will soon be _easier_ (easy) to use than the telephone.

14. Yours is the _lowest_ (low) of the five estimates we received.

15. Of the two semifinalist poems, I think yours is the _better_ (good).

16. The _wettest_ (wet) spring I can remember was in 1992.

17. This cold is even _worse_ (bad) than the one I had last year.

18. Ms. Simms is the _most recent_ (recent) addition to the library staff.

Correct the double negative problems in these sentences. Cross out the error and write the correction above the line.

19. Ted couldn't see ~~no~~ *any* point in staying on the fishing pier past midnight.

20. Hasn't ~~nobody~~ *anybody* called back to return the message?

CHAPTER 17 – TEST B   USING MODIFIERS

In the paragraphs below, circle the modifier that correctly completes each sentence.

(1) My friend Paul is a (real, (really)) cautious person who usually doesn't take risks (easy, (easily)). (2) The (more, (most)) adventurous thing he has ever done was spend a year in England after he finished community college. (3) He (original, (originally)) went to visit a cousin stationed there, but he ended up working at a conference center for almost a year. (4) To this day, Paul appreciates the ((many), more, most) things he learned and experienced during that year.

(5) Even though the British language and culture is similar to America's, Paul soon realized that he was indeed in a different country. (6) For one thing, the weather there was much (damp, (damper), dampest) than in his native Arizona. (7) ((Sudden), Suddenly) rain showers were an almost daily occurrence. (8) The winter he spent was the (worse, (worst)) he could imagine, with the wet cold penetrating his bones. (9) Still, he had to admit he didn't mind the wet weather because England also had the (more, (most)) beautiful gardens he had ever seen. (10) It seemed to him that even the (tiny, tinier, (tiniest)) yard was full of color. (11) Paul became quite a (well, (good)) gardener through his volunteer work in the conference center's garden. (12) His ((previous), previously) training in horticulture was (certain, (certainly)) put to use.

(13) Another difference Paul noticed (quick, (quickly)) was the vocabulary used by his English friends. (14) He (eventual, (eventually)) began to use words such as "Cheerio" and "bloke." (15) He learned that it was ((better), best) to ask the waiter for a "serviette" than for a "napkin" since "nappy" in England refers to a baby's diaper. (16) In a car, one checks the oil under the "bonnet" and puts suitcases in the "boot."

(17) Paul's year in England passed (rapid, (rapidly)). (18) He (final, (finally)) returned home because he missed his girlfriend so (bad, (badly)). (19) Nonetheless, he will always remember this adventure with ((fond), fondest) memories.

CHAPTER 18 – TEST A   CAPITALIZING CORRECTLY

Proofread each sentence below for errors in capitalization. Cross out any errors and write the words correctly above the line.

1. The hurricane had done damage to much of the property at ~~myrtle beach~~ *Myrtle Beach*.

2. How many books have you and your friend ~~susie~~ *Susie* read this summer?

3. I plan to sell these ~~greek~~ *Greek* pastries at the bazaar next ~~saturday~~ *Saturday*.

4. During the ~~korean war~~ *Korean War*, ~~american~~ *American* troops fought under the command of ~~general~~ *General* MacArthur.

5. On ~~thanksgiving day~~ *Thanksgiving Day*, our family will eat dinner at ~~uncle gene's~~ *Uncle Gene's* house.

6. Two of the courses ~~i~~ *I* wanted to take, typing and ~~german~~ *German*, have been canceled.

7. The bombing of the ~~world trade center~~ *World Trade Center* in ~~new york~~ *New York* was an act of terrorism.

8. When I took ~~scott~~ *Scott* to ~~washington,~~ *Washington,* we loved the ~~lincoln memorial~~ *Lincoln Memorial* at dusk.

9. My grandma's favorite meal consists of ~~maine~~ *Maine* lobster and steamed asparagus.

10. Driving southwest across the ~~nevada~~ *Nevada* desert, we were thirsty for ~~gatorade~~ *Gatorade*.

11. The neighborhood known as ~~adams morgan~~ *Adams Morgan* features ethnic diversity; there's even an ~~ethiopian~~ *Ethiopian* restaurant.

12. Hannah's cousin plays her own songs every year at the ~~lone star music festival~~ *Lone Star Music Festival* in ~~austin,~~ *Austin,* ~~texas.~~ *Texas.*

13. The senator will speak to the ~~rotary club~~ *Rotary Club* while on her campaign trip through the ~~south~~ *South*.

14. Did you happen to see the ~~bulls~~ *Bulls* game last night?

15. My uncle teaches several speech classes; his favorite is ~~interpersonal communication~~ *Interpersonal Communication* 162.

16. Shelly's new dog is a ~~maltese~~ *Maltese,* named after an island called ~~malta~~ *Malta,* which is in the ~~mediterranean~~ *Mediterranean* sea.

17. The ~~treaty~~ *Treaty* of ~~ghent~~ *Ghent* ended the ~~war~~ *War* of 1812 between the ~~united states~~ *United States* and ~~great britain~~ *Great Britain*.

18. After high school, Tiffany attended ~~gallaudet university~~ *Gallaudet University* for one year.

19. Newer headache medications such as ~~advil~~ *Advil* and ~~aleve~~ *Aleve* are quite popular.

20. Anyone studying to become a doctor will probably study chemistry and ~~latin~~ *Latin*.

CHAPTER 18 – TEST B   CAPITALIZING CORRECTLY

Proofread the paragraphs below for errors in capitalization. Cross out any errors and write the words correctly above the lines.

(1) My best friend from childhood has a somewhat unusual job for a woman; she's a ~~Truck~~ *truck* driver. (2) Although husband and wife teams are becoming more common, Bonnie drives alone for ~~north~~ *North* American ~~van lines~~ *Van Lines*, a company based in ~~fort wayne, indiana~~ *Fort Wayne, Indiana*. (3) She's been doing this since the days when ~~Truck Stops~~ *truck stops* didn't even offer showers for women. (4) She would either have to ask some other driver to guard the shower or get a room at a ~~days inn~~ *Days Inn* or other motel.

(5) Bonnie got started in her traveling career after her favorite cousin took her in his rig to ~~west point military academy~~ *West Point Military Academy*. (6) They delivered twelve ~~xerox~~ *Xerox* machines to the offices of the ~~School~~ *school* over one ~~labor day~~ *Labor Day* weekend, and she was hooked. (7) Bonnie didn't learn at a certified truck driving school such as ~~new england tractor-trailer academy~~ *New England Tractor Trailer Academy* but on the job as an assistant to a veteran driver. (8) She's well suited to the job because she doesn't mind physical labor, and she's very skilled at dealing with customers as well as her ~~Dispatcher~~ *dispatcher*.

(9) What she likes best, though, is being able to see the ~~Country~~ *country*. (10) She has traveled through forty-five of the states and has often spent extra time in an area. (11) Her favorite destination is the ~~west coast~~ *West Coast*. (12) When she gets a load going westward, she packs her antique ~~schwinn~~ *Schwinn* bicycle in the trailer so she can ride along the ~~pacific~~ *Pacific* after her delivery. (13) Bonnie has learned a great deal of inside information about her job site, ~~america~~ *America*. (14) She knows where to find all the best truck stops, restaurants, backroad short cuts, and ~~Shopping Centers~~ *shopping centers*.

(15) As one might imagine, she has collected a lot of great stories to tell her family when she comes home every ~~christmas~~ *Christmas*. (16) There's the tale of the freak spring snowstorm on the ~~donner pass~~ *Donner Pass* in northern ~~california~~ *California*. (17) Once, she delivered a 2000 year old ~~chinese~~ *Chinese* screen to an art gallery in ~~new york~~ *New York*. (18) Among the interesting people she's met are the former prime minister of ~~england~~ *England* and one of ~~mae west's~~ *Mae West's* boyfriends. (19) Of course, she has been met with lots of surprised looks at loading docks in ~~Companies~~ *companies* across the land. (20) Once they see the quality of her work, however, they have to agree with Bonnie when she says, "~~being~~ *Being* a woman doesn't keep me from doing my job!"

CHAPTER 19 – TEST A   USING PUNCTUATION PROPERLY

Proofread the following sentences for proper punctuation. You may need to add periods, question marks, exclamation points, colons, semicolons, quotation marks, or apostrophes. Insert punctuation as needed above the lines.

1. You must bring several items to the exam: clean paper, a sharpened pencil, and a dictionary.

2. That man's wife asked us if we knew how to change a flat tire.

3. The diver had trained for months; he placed third in the Olympic trials.

4. "Help!" shouted the frightened child at the top of the sliding board.

5. Is that your car rolling down the hill with its lights on?

6. The artist's best work was never seen during his lifetime.

7. "Which movie do you want to go see?" said Sarah to her little brother.

8. If I could invite anyone to dinner, I'd invite only two people: Bill Clinton and Mother Teresa.

9. "Oh, by the way," said Jeremy, "have you ever seen me juggle?"

10. There at the meeting sat Chuck Brown, the lawyer; Janet Tobias, the accountant; and Chris

    Wiley, the chairman of the company.

11. The cat is lying there with its paws crossed around a pencil. What a cute thing!

12. "Who's teaching your stained glass workshop?" asked Dave.

13. A week's vacation may not be enough to get me completely rested.

14. There's not enough sugar in the coffee for Ollie; add another spoonful.

15. George questioned his final grade in the course.

16. Langston Hughes' poem called "Dream Deferred" begins with a question.

17. Nora ran to get help; meanwhile, we moved away from the smoking car.

18. Did the weatherman say when it's supposed to rain?

19. "I'm going off to bed," said the old man.

20. All the golfers' clubs were left in the rain; four bags of clubs were ruined.

CHAPTER 19 – TEST B   USING PUNCTUATION PROPERLY

Proofread the following paragraphs for proper punctuation. Insert periods, questions marks, exclamation points, colons, semicolons, quotation marks, or apostrophes as needed above the lines. If a sentence is correct, write C above it.

(1) If you were born into a home where English was spoken to you in your early years, you learned our language's idioms along with its vocabulary without having to study. (2) Idioms are expressions that have a special meaning beyond the literal meanings of their words; they carry a message different from the meanings of the individual words. (3) For example, consider what it means when someone says to you, "Give me a hand." (4) How can you give someone else a hand?

(5) The native speaker knows that this means to help the person in some way. (6) There are plenty of other examples: under the weather, scratch the surface, frame of mind, to get cold feet.

(7) All of these are expressions that will bring a puzzled look to some students' faces. (8) When you're in a conversation with a friend who speaks English as a second language, watch for that puzzled look; furthermore, watch your own conversation to see how common idioms really are.

(9) Some other potential confusion for speakers of English as a second language can come from a word's multiple meanings. (10) For example, how many different meanings can you think of for the word pick? (11) There are a lot of things a pick can be: a sharp tool used to break up ground, a plastic tool used to play a guitar, or a kind of comb used to groom curly hair. (12) A salesperson might say, "Take your pick," or "We prosecute pickpockets." (13) A mother's advice might include telling her child not to pick at his or her food or not to pick a fight. (14) Do you see how these different uses might confuse a new speaker of English? (15) Think about other words that have several meanings and idiomatic uses: call, put, or take are just a few. (16) Try your best to explain what these sentences mean:

(17) Don't bite my head off.

(18) She's a woman after my own heart.

(19) He was getting in the teacher's hair.

(20) Idioms and various word meanings really make our language interesting and colorful; we just have to be sensitive to our friends who may need a little explanation.

CHAPTER 20 – TEST A   USING COMMAS

Insert commas above the lines as needed in the following sentences.

1. Unless we get some rain soon, the vegetable garden will dry up.

2. Felicia's twin daughters were born on September 30, 1991.

3. Giovanni's, an excellent Italian restaurant, is moving to a new location.

4. We will need to prepare salad, sandwiches, and birthday cake for the picnic.

5. Driving slowly down the icy road, we counted twelve minor accidents.

6. A pet can be a loving companion, but it can also be a big responsibility.

7. She could not, as a matter of fact, remember her old boyfriend's name.

8. They lived in Nome, Alaska, before moving to Tampa, Florida.

9. Her high school softball coach, who had become a dear friend, was retiring.

10. Tell me again, Grandpa, about your experiences in the Great Depression.

11. Edna whispered, "I'll be back in a minute."

12. Leaning too far back in her seat, Kelly tipped over and fell on the floor.

13. Oxford, a city in central England, is best known for its university.

14. After he had finished writing his paper, Pedro took a nap.

15. "I'm sick and tired of tuna for dinner," moaned Terry.

16. On Saturdays Sue works in the yard, goes to the pool, and visits her dad.

17. I can't forget Tuesday, May 7, 1989, when my house burned down.

18. Louis Armstrong, also known as "Satchmo," was a jazz trumpeter and singer.

19. I will not, I repeat, give you permission to borrow my car.

20. Ordinarily, I watch <u>Jeopardy</u> after dinner.

CHAPTER 20 – TEST B   USING COMMAS

Proofread the following paragraphs for missing commas. Insert commas above the lines as needed.

(1) Cathie, a friend of mine from church, really enjoys her work once a month with our local soup kitchen. (2) She has been volunteering there since August 1991, on the first Sunday of every month. (3) Cathie believes in the importance of helping the less fortunate, and she feels good about putting this belief into action. (4) Besides the good feeling she gets from helping others, she appreciates the friendships and sense of teamwork that have developed from working with the same people over time. (5) She feels, as a matter of fact, that she gets as much out of the endeavor as do those they serve.

(6) Every month she is one of the first to arrive and begin setting out chairs, making coffee, or wrapping utensils in napkins. (7) After most of the team of workers has arrived, they have a brief meeting to discuss the day's menu and assign jobs. (8) The meal, which is always well balanced, is planned the day before by a staff dietitian. (9) Menus are based on the food on hand, which is sometimes donated from area restaurants or grocery stores. (10) The captain of the first Sunday team, who has been with the group for twenty years, is very skilled at supervising the process. (11) While some cooks begin to cut vegetables or open cans, others set up the table with salt, pepper, and any other condiment the particular meal calls for. (12) Someone cuts up cakes or pies for dessert, and another volunteer prepares the beverage station. (13) During the preparation time, one of Cathie's regular duties is to count out plates. (14) They know how many plates they start with, and later they count the ones that are left to discover how many people have been served. (15) On a typical Sunday, they serve around three hundred homeless people. (16) Of course, this is a small number compared to that of a city like Washington, DC, or

Los Angeles, California but it's a considerable number for a small Midwestern city like ours.

(17) Cathie's team members try to treat the visitors as they would guests who are eating in their own homes. (18) They welcome diners guide them four at a time to seats and then bring the prepared plates to the table. (19) Trying to maintain eye contact they graciously say "You're quite welcome" when thanked. (20) Cathie along with everyone on her team ends up feeling like a true member of the family of humanity.

CHAPTER 21 – TEST A   MASTERING SPELLING

In the space provided, write the word created by combining the prefix or suffix and the root word as indicated.

1. un + natural =   *unnatural*

2. bear + able =   *bearable*

3. study + ing =   *studying*

4. forget + ing =   *forgetting*

5. re + read =   *reread*

6. commit + ment = *commitment*

7. manage + able = *manageable*

8. lonely + er =   *lonelier*

Circle the correctly spelled word in each pair.

9. breif   / (brief)

10. judgement   / (judgment)

11. (achieve) /   acheive

12. radioes   / (radios)

13. (sufficient) /   sufficeint

Circle the word that correctly completes each sentence.

14. What (affect, (effect)) will this rain have on your picnic plans?

15. The band members will march (past) passed) the principal's box seat.

16. Stan's (conscious, (conscience)) never bothers him, no matter what he does.

17. Paula and Rico's new car is parked over (their, (there)).

18. Izzy cannot remember (were, (where)) she left her notebook.

19. ((Your, You're)) welcome in our house any time.

20. I do not feel that I ought to (except, (accept)) that money.

CHAPTER 21 – TEST B   MASTERING SPELLING

In the blanks, supply the missing words by putting together the parts given in parentheses.

(1) Over the past few decades, there has been a growing (commit + ment) _commitment_ to taking care of our earth. (2) Even young children are (worry + ing) _worrying_ these days about protecting the environment. (3) Much has (occur + ed) _occurred_ to help each of us know how to help. (4) Books such as _Fifty Simple Things You Can Do to Save the Earth_ show us how to make environmental protection a part of our (day + ly) _daily_ lives. (5) None of us can close up the hole in the ozone layer, but all of us can make it our (busy + ness) _business_ to stop using the chlorofluorocarbons (CFCs) that worsen the ozone problem. (6) Each of us is (response + ible) _responsible_.

(7) One thing that many families already do is (re + cycle) _recycle_. (8) Many communities have programs that provide convenient containers, which makes saving newspaper or glass quite (manage + able) _manageable_. (9) To save water, never leave the tap (run + ing) _running_ when you wash dishes or brush your teeth. (10) Picking up trash as you find it in the neighborhood sets a good example and makes your surroundings more (beauty + ful) _beautiful_.

Cross out each misspelled word and write the word correctly above the line.

(11) The things ~~your~~ _you're_ able to do around your home are not only easy but also economical. (12) Saving energy saves money, and it might also save frustration to make your home less ~~clutterred~~ _cluttered_. (13) One way to do this is to stop ~~recieving~~ _receiving_ so much junk mail. (14) To do this, write to Mail Preference Service; its address is Direct Marketing Association, 11 West 42nd Street, PO Box 3861, New York, NY 10163-3861. (15) Another way to reduce paper is ~~too~~ _to_ use your own cloth or string bag when you shop. (16) That way, when the clerk asks, "Paper or plastic?" you can reply, "~~Niether~~ _Neither_!" (17) ~~Their~~ _There_ are certain kinds of packaging you should avoid ~~completly~~ _completely_, such as foam. (18) ~~Its~~ _It's_ easy to save ~~alot~~ _a lot_ of water when flushing the toilet by placing a plastic bottle in the tank to

displace some of the water the tank will hold. (19) Taking care of our planet is everyone's job.

(20) Anyone ~~whose~~ *who's* not part of the solution is part of the problem.

CHAPTER 22 – TEST A   MAINTAINING PARALLELISM

In each group, circle the part that is not parallel with the rest.

1. Chinese eggrolls
   (bread from France)
   Greek salad
   Mexican tacos

2. (to go home)
   to the bank
   to the drycleaners
   to the drug store

3. who was ready
   who was prepared
   who was patient
   (who had an air of confidence)

4. cute
   funny
   (with wealth)
   tall

In the sentences below, fill in each blank with a word or phrase that will maintain parallel structure in the sentence.

ANSWERS WILL VARY.

5. My hobbies include hunting, fishing, and _camping_.

6. Janet usually wants to go out on weekends while her husband _wants to stay home_.

7. You look very _cheerful_ and _rested_ today.

8. At the gift shop, we bought Dad a book and _a CD_.

9. To get to the cabin from here, go across the field and _over the bridge_.

10. Her motto is "Look good, act tough, and _talk straight_."

11. Attend class, sit up front, and _take notes_ if you want to succeed in college.

12. Uncle Jed's old truck shook, sputtered, and _died_.

Change words or phrases to make the following sentences parallel. Cross out errors, and write your corrections above the lines.

ANSWERS MAY VARY SLIGHTLY.

13. In the oath of office, the President swears to preserve, *to* protect, and to defend the Constitution of the United States.

14. My vacation this summer had all the best ingredients: beautiful view, great companionship, and the ~~weather was sunny~~ *sunny weather*.

15. Whoever gets this job will have to be conscientious, friendly, and ~~with a sense of responsibility~~ *responsible*.

16. From the window she could see the corn fields, the ~~barn that was old,~~ *old barn,* and the distant hills ~~were in view too~~.

17. Luke is a student, a businessman, and ~~he has two kids~~ *a father*.

18. By driving all night, eating in the car and ~~we only stopped~~ *stopping only* to fill up with gas, we were able to reach Detroit by noon.

19. Arnold Arboretum is a good place ~~for a walk~~ *to walk* or to teach kids about trees.

20. Carol has decided to be either a nurse or ~~she might like to teach school~~ *a teacher*.

CHAPTER 22 – TEST B   MAINTAINING PARALLELISM

Proofread the following paragraphs for parallel structure. Cross out any errors, and write the corrections above the lines as needed. For sentences 12 and 17, write in the blanks sentence beginnings that will be parallel to the sentence beginning of the second paragraph (sentence 5). **ANSWERS MAY VARY SLIGHTLY.**

(1) America's diverse mixture of ethnic backgrounds and communities has caused the country to be called a melting pot or a ~~bowl with salad in it~~ *salad bowl*. (2) Just as our population is quite varied, our language also contains a wide range of varying word uses, word origins, and ~~expressions that are regional.~~ *regional expressions.* (3) Learning the stories behind word origins can help a student learn new vocabulary, *and remember* ~~and remembering new vocabulary is easier too~~. (4) Besides, it can be fun to learn about words or try~~ing~~ out new words in conversations.

(5) One way our language adds new words is to borrow from other languages. (6) Many of the individual words that appear in an American dictionary originated in foreign languages. (7) In addition to these, we are beginning to borrow more and more conversational expressions from other languages. (8) For example, most of us know how to say and ~~we have the~~ understand~~ing of~~ the word "goodbye" in several languages. (9) "Adios" is Spanish, "ciao" is Italian, and "Cheerio" ~~comes from Britain~~ *is British*. (10) We say "Bon voyage!" when someone leaves for a trip or "Eureka!" ~~is what we can say~~ when we find or realize something. (11) We might describe a friend as having "chutzpah," which is Yiddish, or as having "wanderlust," which ~~comes from the~~ *is* German.

(12) Another _____*way our language adds new words is*_____ to borrow from science or technology. (13) Many of these new words are acronyms, which are formed from the first letters of a title or string of words. (14) Reading the newspaper, listening to the radio, or ~~when we watch~~ *watching* TV, we might encounter words such as "NATO" or "SALT." (15) Everyone knows what a "yuppie" or a "zip" code is even though the words they come from may not be as

familiar. (16) Those who study computers or ~~working~~ in the computer field know abut "DOS"

and "RAM."

(17) Still ___*another way our language adds new words is*___ to borrow

from literature or legend. (18) For example, a myth tells of a man in Hades who was tortured by

the gods. (19) He was forced to stand in a pool of cool water that disappeared whenever he bent

to drink; overhead were branches of wonderful fruit ~~blowing out of reach with him trying to eat~~. *that blew out of reach when he tried to eat.*

(20) His name was Tantalus, and this is where we get the word "tantalize."

MASTERY TEST

Circle the letter of the choice that best completes the sentence or gives a correct statement about the sentence.

Section 1: Subject and Verbs, Fragments, Subordination, Coordination, Run-ons, and Comma Splices

1. The cataloging of books in this library is presently being converted to the computer system.
    - A. subject = books   &   verb = is being
    - (B.) subject = cataloging   &   verb = is being converted
    - C. subject = library   &   verb = is being converted

2. One of the exercise bicycles needs a new seat.
    - (A.) subject = one   &   verb = needs
    - B. subject = exercise   &   verb = needs
    - C. subject = bicycles   &   verb = needs

3. An understanding of world history will help students in many ways.
    - A. subject = history   &   verb = help
    - B. subject = history   &   verb = will help
    - (C.) subject = understanding &   verb = will help

4. Ken's car had been thoroughly inspected and tuned up before the trip.
    - A. subject = Ken's   &   verb = had been inspected
    - B. subject = car   &   verb = had been thoroughly inspected
    - (C.) subject = car   &   verb = had been inspected, tuned

5. It saddened her greatly.
    - (A.) The group of words is a sentence.
    - B. The group of words is not a sentence.

6. Dan so astonished that he couldn't speak to anyone at the surprise party.
    - A. The group of words is a sentence.
    - (B.) The group of words is not a sentence.

7. Trying to catch a glimpse of the movie stars in the restaurant, he walked backwards.
    - (A.) The group of words is a sentence.
    - B. The group of words is not a sentence.

8. While I was at home waiting for the plumber to come repair the sink.
    - A. The group of words is a sentence.
    - (B.) The group of words is not a sentence.

9. Hannah wasn't allowed to go to the _____ she had lied to her mom.
    A. beach, because
    B. beach although
    C. beach because

10. _____ Jose moved to Maine, he had never seen the ocean.
    A. Unless
    B. Until
    C. While

11. Hannah enrolled in _____ her daughter said she was too old.
    A. college although
    B. college, although
    C. college; although

12. Vimla wanted to be a _____ she changed her major from music to foods.
    A. chef and
    B. chef so
    C. chef, so

13. At first I was just _____ I became angry.
    A. upset, then
    B. upset, and then
    C. upset and then

14. Andrew proposed to her in _____ was very romantic.
    A. Paris; it
    B. Paris since
    C. Paris and

15. "I'm just about ready, make yourself at home," said Debbie.
    A. The sentence is correct.
    B. There is a problem that needs correcting.

16. The dog was barking loudly as if he had seen a stranger.
    A. The sentence is correct.
    B. There is a problem that needs correcting.

17. The food ran out before the party was _____ we had to order pizza.
    A. over, we
    B. over we
    C. over; we

Section 2: Verbs, Voice, Tenses, and Consistency

18. Mark cracks his knuckles all the _____ irritates his girlfriend.
    A. time this
    B. time, and this
    C. time, this

19. One of my neighbors _____ his lawn every day all day long.
    A. water
    B. waters
    C. watered

20. I think Mom and Dad _____ the anniversary party we are planning.
    A. will enjoy
    B. enjoy
    C. are enjoying

21. By working overtime last month, the club members _____ enough money to give the coach a nice gift at his retirement party.
    A. saving
    B. will save
    C. had saved

22. Have you _____ much money to charities this year?
    A. gave
    B. given

23. Hilda feels that her husband _____ far too much on her birthday gift.
    A. has spended
    B. have spent
    C. has spent

24. When I saw the ice cream truck go by, I _____ after it.
    A. ran
    B. run
    C. will run

25. At the lake last summer, my kids _____ several interesting rocks.
    A. finding
    B. found
    C. find

26. Chuck _____ his lunch every day, but he never _____ it.
    A. brings . . . ate
    (B.) brings . . . eats
    C. has brought . . . ate

27. Jackson and Sons Contracting Company built our new house.
    (A.) This sentence has a verb in the active voice.
    B. This sentence has a verb in the passive voice.

28. When the phone rang, I _____ into the shower.
    A. stepped
    B. am stepping
    (C.) was stepping

29. Vickie says that she _____ give me a ride to the airport next Wednesday.
    A. would
    (B.) will
    C. could

30. The clowns _____ silly, and their antics are making the children laugh.
    A. were
    B. will be
    (C.) are being

Section 3: Nouns, Pronouns, and Modifiers

31. The bank's telephone system allows you to transfer money between _____.
    A. account
    (B.) accounts

32. My grandmother has given most of her china to my sister and _____.
    (A.) me
    B. I
    C. myself

33. Sonia is a good dancer, but Carlos can dance better than _____ can.
    A. her
    B. hers
    (C.) she

34. Chris and _____ are going to the business meeting together.
    (A.) I
    B. me
    C. us

35. Somebody forgot to clean up _____ own mess.
    Ⓐ. his or her
    B. their
    C. our

36. Everyone was stunned when the jury returned _____ verdict.
    A. their
    Ⓑ. its

37. Cigarettes are hazardous to your health and expensive. _____ are two reasons to try to quit smoking.
    A. That
    B. This
    Ⓒ. These

38. Books that _____ well worn and well read usually stand the test of time.
    A. is
    Ⓑ. are

39. Michael washes dishes _____ than anyone else in our family.
    A. most careful
    B. most carefully
    Ⓒ. more carefully

40. The reason Irina is such a _____ administrator is that she listens _____.
    Ⓐ. good . . . well
    B. good . . . good
    C. well . . . good

41. Marta was the _____ person I ever roomed with, and she was the _____ cook, too!
    A. most messy . . . worst
    B. messiest . . . worse
    Ⓒ. messiest . . . worst

42. The Underwood family _____ ends meet since their home burned; our church is helping them.
    Ⓐ. can hardly make
    B. can't hardly make

Section 4: Punctuation, Capitals, Spelling and Parallel Structure

43. While Owen was driving _____, he had two flat tires.
    - (A.) south to Stone Mountain
    - B. South to Stone Mountain
    - C. south to Stone mountain

44. Hugo was so angry that he threatened to write a letter to _____.
    - A. governor Whitman
    - (B.) Governor Whitman

45. For _____ Walter gave his _____ a hammock.
    - A. Fathers' day . . . dad
    - (B.) Fathers' Day . . . dad
    - C. Fathers' Day . . . Dad

46. The _____ had been stolen from their unlocked trucks, so they all had to buy new ones.
    - A. carpenter's tools
    - B. carpenters tools'
    - (C.) carpenters' tools

47. "Where is my favorite _____ scowled Mr. Bostwick.
    - (A.) pen?"
    - B. pen"?
    - C. pen,"

48. The committee is made up of representatives from four _____ Hillsdale, Gillespie, and Deerfield.
    - A. towns, Conway,
    - B. towns; Conway,
    - (C.) towns: Conway,

49. _____ screamed Ed as his wife drove off with his only house key.
    - A. "Wait,"
    - (B.) "Wait!"
    - C. "Wait"!

50. Teaching her son to fix his own _____ learned a few things herself about patience.
    - A. breakfast Fran
    - (B.) breakfast, Fran
    - C. breakfast; Fran

51. Ernie's grandfather remembers _____ the happiest day of his life.
    A. April 17, 1956, as
    B. April 17, 1956 as
    C. April, 17, 1956,

52. The sequoia tree resists damage from _____ and lives to be very old and large.
    A. fungus, insects and fire
    B. fungus, insects, and fire,
    C. fungus, insects, and fire

53. The Willamette River, which flows north through Corvallis and _____ the Columbia near Portland.
    A. Albany, joins
    B. Albany joins
    C. Albany; joins

54. The _____ are cooking fast; please add some more water to the pan.
    A. potatoes
    B. potatos

55. Next month, the Wongs will be _____ back to a family reunion in Idaho.
    A. traveling
    B. travelling

56. Most people feel it is rude to criticize a person for his or her _____.
    A. believes
    B. beleifs
    C. beliefs

57. _____ willing to go _____ or not we take the air-conditioned van?
    A. Whose . . . weather
    B. Whose . . . whether
    C. Who's . . . whether

58. His hobby of collecting antique cars is harmless but _____.
    A. the expense is great
    B. expensive
    C. it takes a lot of money

59. Being chairperson of our committee will require your time, your energy, and _____.
    A. commitment
    B. your commitment
    C. the ability to be committed

60. She understands what needs to be done but not _____.
    Ⓐ. how to do it
    B. knowing how it should be done
    C. the way to do it

MASTERY TEST ITEM ANALYSIS

Test Items Missed				Chapter/Skill		#Correct/# on test
1	2	3	4	5	Subjects & Verbs	_____ / 4
5	6	7	8	6	Sentence Fragments	_____ / 4
9	10	11		7	Subordination	_____ / 3
12	13	14		8	Coordination	_____ / 3
15	16	17	18	9	Comma Splice & Run-On	_____ / 4
19	20	21		11	Regular Verbs	_____ / 3
22	23	24	25	12	Irregular Verbs	_____ / 4
26	27	28		13	Passive, Prog., Consistency	_____ / 3
29	30	31		14	Additional Verb Use	_____ / 3
32	33	34	35	15	Nouns & Pronouns	_____ / 4
36	37	38	39	16	Pronoun-Antecedent Agreement	_____ / 4
40	41	42		17	Modifiers	_____ / 3
43	44	45		18	Capitals	_____ / 3
46	47	48	49	19	Punctuation	_____ / 4
50	51	52	53	20	Commas	_____ / 4
54	55	56	57	21	Spelling	_____ / 4
58	59	60		22	Parallelism	_____ / 3

Total
Correct =   _____ / 60

NOTES

NOTES

NOTES

NOTES

NOTES

NOTES

NOTES

NOTES

NOTES

NOTES

NOTES

NOTES

NOTES

NOTES

NOTES